What They Don't Always Teach You at a Christian College

With Questions for Groups

KEITH ANDERSON

InterVarsity Press
Downers Grove, Illinois

InterVarsity Press® is the book-publishing division of InterVarsity Christian Fellowship®, a student movement active on campus at hundreds of universities, colleges and schools of nursing in the United States of America, and a member movement of the International Fellowship of Evangelical Students. For information about local and regional activities, write Public Relations Dept., InterVarsity Christian Fellowship, 6400 Schroeder Rd., P.O. Box 7895, Madison, WI 53707-7895.

All Scripture quotations, unless otherwise indicated, are taken from the New Revised Standard Version of the Bible, copyright 1989 by the Division of Christian Education of the National Council of the Churches of Christ in the U.S.A., and are used by permission.

"Moonrise" excerpt from The Ministry of the Child by Dennis C. Benson and Stan Stewart (Recycle Press, 6463 Lakeshore Drive, West Olive, Michigan 49460). Copyright 1978, 1979, 1992. Used with permission.

ISBN 0-8308-1611-9

Printed in the United States of America

Library of Congress Cataloging-in-Publication Data

Anderson, Keith R., 1949-
 What they don't always teach you at a Christian college/Keith R.
Anderson.
  p.   cm.
 Includes bibliographical references.
 ISBN 0-8308-1611-9 (pbk.: alk. paper)
  1. College students—Religious life. 2. College students—Conduct
of life. 3. Christian life. 4. Church colleges. I. Title.
BV4531.2.A4 1995
248.8'34—dc20   95-16658
                                                                   CIP

21   20   19   18   17   16   15   14   13   12   11   10   9   8   7   6

12   11   10   09   08   07   06   05   04   03   02   01   00

For my parents, who live what they say they believe.
For my children, Kevin, Keri and Kristoffer,
who daily bring God's grace to my life.
For Wendy, whose love makes it all possible.

Acknowledgments

My teachers have been many—starting with my family, good friends and colleagues. But it has been my students, both in and outside of the classroom, whose honest and sometimes ruthless questions have carried truth to me most powerfully.

☐ The patient students who helped me grow in my early years of teaching beginning at Sioux Falls College and continuing each day at Bethel.

☐ The many individuals, discipleship groups and worship teams with whom I walked in many places.

☐ "The guys" who are there to keep me accountable.

☐ The many students who have participated in the Chicago courses over the years.

My staff at Bethel, who have created a place of hospitality for growth and ministry beyond any of our expectations—Steve, Sherry, Carmen and Elaine, who patiently live with me in the hours of humor, joy and pain in Campus Ministries.

My co-thinker and treasured friend Kirby Wilcoxson, with whom I wrestle with real questions.

Dave Brandt, who has given me what few can give—unconditional love and confidence that gives wings to my ministry.

And my sister and brother chaplains and campus pastors in the Christian College Coalition, who refine and sharpen the work as iron sharpens iron.

To all of you and many more, I can only say, "Here are my mother and my brothers! For whoever does the will of my Father in heaven is my brother and sister and mother."

Foreword

I was sitting at my desk at the Youth for Christ national headquarters in Wheaton, Illinois, when the phone rang. At the other end was the familiar voice of a nationally known speaker and lecturer. He said, "Jay, I'm at Wheaton College doing a Staley Lecture to the student body, and I'm dying! What will turn these students on?" We laughed together a little nervously and agreed to have a cup of coffee and discuss his dilemma. My suggestion to him was to quit trying to impress the faculty with his academic background and to ignore his own growing edge and ask the question, "What was it like to be a college student and what were the mega-themes on your mind during those days? Speak to these themes." He said, "That seems so basic," to which I replied, "That's the point. Each generation must go through its own rite of passage, but the path from adolescence to adulthood remains somewhat the same."

Keith Anderson helps us with this age-old challenge, that is, the task of facing the issues that all must deal with in the maturation process while acknowledging the unique challenges of contemporary society. This book will prove a valuable guide to college students faced with a historic faith and a modern world. This is not a preachy book, but a patient one that squarely faces the challenges but allows enough percolation time for today's students to process the ideas.

Anderson deals daily with students, so he knows the issues. He is also a chaplain and minister, so he knows the destination of faith. This is a book to help students become self-regulating young adults committed to Jesus Christ, not out of a sense of obligation but out of thoughtful, committed love.

Jay Kesler

1

The Great
Adventure Begins

I t's the beginning of a new school year, your first days on campus. What a whirlwind! In just a couple of days you have moved in, met people whose names you've already forgotten, registered for classes, joined several groups and gone to several picnics or banquets. You've been oriented and *dis*oriented. All of this and you haven't even started classes yet!

My own introduction to college life was very traumatic. I was excited, but I was also pretty shy—actually, very shy. And the "Welcome Week" staff made me feel even more shy—and irritated.

My orientation started with wearing the required atrocious green "freshman beanie" day and night for the first week of school. Any upperclass student could stop us at any given time and force us to "button." This meant that we had to place our index finger on the top of the beanie and recite the freshman chant "OH WHA TA GOO SIAM," spinning around in a circle as we said it. Now that was something to look forward to with excitement! (If someone had told me about those beanies, I might have gone to college somewhere else!)

Another orientation activity was the freshman retreat. I remember the bus ride to the camp very well. I was miserable. I only knew two people on the entire campus, and they were nowhere to be found. People didn't exactly seek me out to talk to me, and I was equally hesitant to talk to them. I barely talked to anyone until a beautiful, blue-eyed female student asked me a deeply personal and intimate question: "Is this the bus to the freshman retreat?" I didn't leave her side until we returned to campus two days later! Orientation was tough on me!

I felt so uptight about the trauma of beginning that school year and meeting new people that at one point I hid out in a bathroom stall in the gym. I can remember saying out loud, "I'll be glad when it's November and all of this new stuff is behind me."

For some of you the beginning of college will be equally traumatic. For others of you it will be the greatest day of your life—Christmas, your birthday and the Fourth of July all rolled into one. It will be exactly what you've been waiting for all of your life. All you have to do is survive while your parents help you settle in.

Every fall students tell me it feels like "The Brady Bunch Goes to College." It's bad enough that your parents had to come with you, but they actually brought your brother and sister along! Now your mother is putting your socks in your drawer, and your father is building a loft for your bed. Your little sister is convinced that you need her to stay with you, and she's crying. Your brother is down in the lounge trying to pick up dates for *your* homecoming. You only hope no one knows they're your relatives.

The first days on campus mark an important time for every new class of students. God loves "beginnings"—creation and new creation, birth and new birth, new heaven and new earth. The great Jewish writer Elie Wiesel once said, "When God created man, God gave him a secret— and that secret was not how to begin, but how to begin again."

As you look at the new academic year ahead, you stand on the edge of a "new beginning." There are new friendships to build and new places to see, perhaps even a new city to learn as well as a new campus to discover. And who is that person who now lives on the other side of the room from you? There's a lot to learn during this time of orientation.

It will also be a time of *dis*orientation. During your first few weeks on campus, you may not be sure if you're coming or going—and not sure how to get there anyway. You're not alone in those feelings of being rushed and of racing through the first weeks of school. Many share these feelings of confusion and apprehension. You may begin to feel it closing in on you every time you have to go to a new class in a new building. Or you may feel it every time you walk into the dining center and look around for someone familiar. There are too many forms, too many lines, too many new things all at once.

The early days of the semester are known for their rapid pace and the confusion they often create, but that's probably nothing new for you. Each year of your life a ritual has been repeated. Since you were a small child you have experienced this cycle of life; it is the beginning of the school year. Perhaps you made the transition from a day care to a preschool, then a preschool to an elementary school, to a junior high or middle school, and finally into high school. You made it through those transitions, and now as a college student you are about to start all over again.

Saying Hello

In the early months of this century, a young Swedish immigrant named Peter stood on Ellis Island waiting in line to be processed into the country that would one day be his. He clutched his hat in his hands (as I saw him do many times in his later years), and he looked on this vast new land and dreamed great dreams for this place. I learned much from my immigrant grandfather, and I have often reflected on his life as a metaphor for times of change in my own.

Today you too stand on the shores of a new land, a new place in your history, and dream great dreams. At the beginning of a great adventure like college, you don't know what God will do *with* you, *through* you, *to* you and probably *in spite of* you! Like my immigrant grandfather, you have much to learn. Saying hello to a new country, or to a new place, or even to a new time in your life means that you will learn a new language. The language of the academic community will stretch you and require frequent trips to that dictionary Uncle Fred gave you for graduation!

Saying hello means that you will learn a new culture. Your dorm, apartment or residence hall has its own culture, its own ways, its own particular patterns of life. Some of you will discover that the college student day is often just beginning at eleven o'clock at night!

Saying hello means that you will learn new disciplines. One of the most important lessons to be learned (or missed) in the first semester of college life is a strange new art form called "time management." Remember to take time to plan your weeks and examine your use of time. Become friends with your syllabi and your calendar. Sit down with your calendar and fill in all the due dates for exams and papers. Set your priorities well.

Saying hello is something that continues all through our lives. In a wonderful sense, we are always beginners. God seems to want it that way, because we are allowed to begin again and again.

What lies before you now is a vast canvas on which you will paint the new portrait of your life as a college student. Your choices are many and your opportunities are great. You can paint a picture using the same old color you've always used before, or you can open up to the whole rainbow of colors and paint your life in glorious new shades. You can copy someone else's picture and draw only what you see around you, making a picture that is as mass-produced as the morning paper, or you and God can paint a picture the world has never seen before— the picture of *your* life, *your* faith, *your* walk with God. Remember the great line of the *Star Trek* series? "To boldly go where no man has ever gone before." That can be you too.

This book is written with a simple assumption: Kingdom thinking is the absolutely essential enterprise for Christian students. It is a way of thinking that is specific to women and men who are committed to the kingdom of God. It is a way of thinking that is biblically based and sensitive to God's Spirit. Kingdom thinking shapes students into active participants in the kingdom of God.

Some students are able to do such thinking in the classrooms of Christian colleges and universities. For them this "integration of faith and learning" is a natural part of the curriculum and experience at their schools. For many other Christian students, this kind of thinking will be done apart from classroom content and professors' input. This book is designed to help students in both situations find their way through the school year. Some parts of this book are very practical and outline steps and methods; other parts ask you to consider issues and to come up with your own thinking and answers.

I once had a wise professor say to me, "Don't let your classes get in the way of your education." He meant that education is an all-encompassing enterprise that occurs in all the times and places that learning takes place. The word *education* comes from the Latin word *educare*, which means to draw out, to discover and to see the world in new ways or with new eyes, to *educe* the truth that lies within.

My introduction to the real world of college life was rough. But I lived through it, and I know you will too. After all, *you* don't have to wear a beanie everywhere you go!

Questions for Groups

1. Tell each other your best memory about a "first day of school" as a child. What made it so great?

2. Describe your most embarrassing "first day of school" from childhood.

3. What has been the best part of your transition into this new school year?

4. Ask how you can pray for each other in these days of transition into this new school year.

2

Begin Where You Are

I remember very well my first day in Sunday school in second grade. We had moved that summer, and I was the new kid. I left the comfortable, friendly confines of the familiar "old" church, as it came to be called, to find myself at the "new" church. Familiar names like Uncle Bob and Mr. Whitoff gave way to new people with strange, unfamiliar names like Broderick, Baptista, Caldwell, Forester and Wareham.

I sat very straight and tall in the little blue chairs as the new teacher welcomed the class. (At least, I tried to be tall. It was tough because I was a micro-child in second grade. In fact, I was a micro-child until the eleventh grade. Thankfully, I didn't know that then.) Even in my micro-suit and micro-bow tie and best micro-white shirt, I was scared. This was new, and I didn't know if I would ever like it as much as the old church. I didn't know what to feel—I was very excited, but very scared. Would these taller classmates like me, or at least not hurt me? They seemed so comfortable there. They even knew the answer to one of my most immediate concerns, the answer to the all-important question: "Where is the boys' bathroom?"

Well, I asked and found my way, and I'm sure the bow tie was perfect and my butchwaxed crewcut was flat and straight when I walked back toward my classroom. As I walked past the wooden dividers between the primary and junior class, I heard a sound that was familiar. A song. One I knew, for we sang it at the old church and I liked it.

The wise man built his house upon the rock.
The wise man built his house upon the rock.
The wise man built his house upon the rock.
And the rains came tumbling down.

I've never forgotten that song.

Some of you may feel like that kid in the bow tie and flattop, scared feelings and all. You're excited, not sure what's going to happen next, anticipating but still a little anxious. One reason I told you this story is to acknowledge that feelings will abound at the beginning of a new year. Life will tumble in and around you in these next days, and your feelings will scramble to keep up with it all.

But there is another reason for this story: Jesus told the parable contained in that song to help us ask life's most important questions: Who or what will be the authority for my life? Who or what will I follow, obey and trust? The parable points us to the only solid foundation for our lives—Jesus Christ.

On the Edge

As a student you stand on the precipice of the greatest opportunity you may ever have in your life—the opportunity for an adventuresome walk with Jesus Christ. You can have four years of some of life's richest opportunities for learning and loving and serving and growing. These can be some of the best years you've ever had for becoming educated in the kingdom of God.

It takes intentionality to name Jesus as Lord. You have to do that on purpose. It takes intentionality to grow. A secondhand faith doesn't cut it. An inherited faith doesn't cut it. Neither does the faith of your parents or of your church. Now is the time, and college is the place, to choose it for yourself. Many people follow Jesus halfway, but not the whole way. Many admire Jesus—from a distance. Tony Campolo says that there are plenty of college-student Christians today who hang back, waiting to see if it's "cool" to be "hot" about following Jesus.

Picture Your Future

Among the questions I hope you will answer in the early weeks of your first semester is this one: How much of myself am I going to give to the kingdom of God?

Use your imagination for just a moment. Visualize the "house" of your life nine or ten months from now.

☐ What do you want your life to look like?

☐ Whom do you want to be?

☐ What values will you have?

☐ What priorities will be yours?

☐ What goals will you set?

We build our lives decision by decision, day by day, step by step. Where and how do you begin? In *A Testament of Devotion*, Thomas Kelly gives his answer: "Begin where you are. Obey now. Use what little obedience you are capable of, even if it be like a grain of mustard seed. Begin where you are."

Calvin and Hobbes are the characters (a boy and his "stuffed" tiger) in a popular comic strip by Bill Watterson. In one strip they are hurtling down a hill in a small wagon, and Calvin says to Hobbes, "Ever notice how decisions make chain reactions?" Hobbes asks, "How so?" "Well," says Calvin, "each decision we make determines the range of choices we'll face next. Take this fork in the road for instance. Which way should we go? Arbitrarily, I choose left. Now, as a direct result of that decision, we're faced with another choice: Should we jump this ledge or ride along the side of it? If we hadn't turned left at the fork, this new choice would never have come up."

At this point the wagon has launched into midair, and Hobbes says with alarm, "I note, with some dismay, you've chosen to jump the ledge." "Right," replies Calvin. "And *that* decision will give us *new* choices." Still in midair, Hobbes asks, "Like, should we bail out or die in the landing?" "Exactly," answers Calvin. "Our first decision created a chain reaction of decisions. Let's jump."

The little boy and the tiger jump from the wagon and land in a stream, where Calvin continues his philosophical reflection. "See? If you don't make each decision carefully, you never know *where* you'll end up. That's an important lesson we should learn sometime."

Hobbes, soaking wet and more than a little upset, says, "I wish we could talk about these things without the visual aids."

Jesus said that the choice of authority we make has a dramatic impact on the twists and turns of our lives. Following Jesus is something you decide to do. You say yes over and over and over again.

Don't Even Think of Parking Here

I was at Princeton University a few years ago and found myself walking down Nassau Street. This beautiful street has a lively sense of history, dignity and importance. Albert Einstein and other important shapers of history once lived on Nassau Street. Like many of the streets in that part of town, however, it is narrow, old and overcrowded—parking is a real problem. There, in jarring juxtaposition to the beauty of ivy and gothic architecture, was a sign nailed to a house, obviously written by an irate homeowner tired of sharing his driveway with the world: "Don't Even Think of Parking Here."

It's a great thought that can help keep the fires of motivation lit all during the year, but especially as you begin the year. If you are new in the faith, there is much to learn. To you the words are a robust challenge: Don't Even Think of Parking Here. If you are veterans of the faith: Don't Even Think of Parking Here. If you think you know it, if you believe you have it all put together, if your mind is made up and closed, the challenge is clear: Reopen your heart and mind. Don't Even Think of Parking Here.

In J. R. R. Tolkien's Lord of the Rings, Frodo sets out on a great mission that he doesn't want and for which he feels terribly inadequate.

An overwhelming longing to rest and remain at peace by Bilbo's side in Rivendell filled all his heart. At last with an effort he spoke, and wondered to hear his own words, as if some other will was using his small voice.

"I will take the Ring," he said, "though I do not know the way."
That is faith. That is the road, the path, the way that will lead to growth.

To Will One Will

The name Jim Elliot is important to an entire generation of Christians who knew him as one of the five young missionaries martyred at the hands of the Auca Indians in Ecuador. He became a model to many, a hero of faith because of his courageous determination to follow Christ with 100 percent of his life. One of my student friends, Scott, has also come to see Elliot as his hero of faith—not only for his courage in his missions work but also for his single-minded obedience, which began when Jim Elliot was a college student. He started well. He built a solid foundation and learned discipline early. And because of that his life and his words have been mightily used by God.

Scott's passionate interest in the life of Jim Elliot sent me back to his life and writings, where I rediscovered the secret to the power of his faith. He is probably best known for a statement from the book *Shadow of the Almighty*: "He is no fool who gives what he cannot keep to gain what he cannot lose." Elisabeth Elliot wrote of him as a college student: "It was his singleness of purpose that his fellow students noticed especially." It takes courage and determination to become a fully alive follower of Jesus Christ. It means you say yes again and again and again.

Almost as soon as you arrive at your school, you will hear voices anxious to attract your attention and your allegiance. Always ask yourself if these voices are worthy foundations for centering your life. You will choose something to be the priority, the central focus, of your semester. So keep the main thing the main thing. Remember, the Christian life is not a sprint but a long-distance run.

Questions for Groups

1. With whom did you identify most—Calvin or Hobbes?
2. Write out three goals that you want to set for your spiritual growth in the year ahead. Share one of these goals with the group.
3. Identify the "voices" you have heard on campus that have excited your interest. Why do you feel drawn to these particular people, groups or activities? In what way do you think these will contribute to your growth this year?
4. Ask each other how the group can pray for you this week.

3

Pick Your Fights

Over the past few years I have met with many parents during orientation week. I usually share with them the following letter, which I received some years ago.

Dear Keith:

As the concerned parent of a newly matriculating freshman, I'd like to outline my goals for my son.

I look forward to his return at Thanksgiving as a fully mature, well-rounded, spiritually vibrant, physically well, young man.

Neal has never been a consistent person in his devotional life, so I am glad you will train him to study the scriptures in a disciplined fashion. I know your chapels are especially inspiring, so I trust you will be able to get him to chapel each week, even though we couldn't get him to attend church regularly with our family.

He has never been a particularly neat and tidy person, so I know your housing staff will be able to assist him in keeping his residence hall room clean and always well-kept.

(By the way, we forgot to teach him how to do laundry, so I thank you in advance for taking time to teach him that skill.)

He hasn't been particularly adept as a student in his high school years, so I hope your faculty will teach him how to study, in fact, it would be nice if you would find someone to teach him how to read.

His writing in cursive isn't very good either, could you assist in that development?

Neal has never eaten well-rounded meals at home, so please work on his diet so he comes home ready to eat all the vegetables he hated at our home.

Neal has never participated in sports, music, or theater, so I'd like you to get him involved in one fall sport, the Bethel choir, and then a winter play—a leading role would be nice, but would that be too much to ask?

Neal is somewhat shy, so I look forward to your help in getting him his first date and then making sure all goes well on that date.

Finally, I would like you to help him find a part-time job, preferably in computers at $10/hour and then please provide transportation for him to and from work.

This father didn't want just some normal growth for his son—his goal was major reconstruction! Most students' parents set some kind of goals for their children. Those goals that others set for you are important, but most important are the goals that are your own. The exciting and perhaps scary fact before you now is that you have some important decisions to make and some goals of your own to set.

The New Testament offers three simple directions to help you set those priorities. Paul said, "I have fought the good fight, I have finished the race, I have kept the faith." This is not just ancient wisdom, it is very practical help for today!

Fight the Good Fight

You can choose to fight many battles in the year ahead. But which ones? Choose to fight the *good* fight, Paul would say. That is, choose your battles carefully. Some battles are unnecessary. Some we drift into because we are not alert; others we choose out of rebellion or emotional hurt.

Every year I watch students make decisions that take them into battles they need not fight: battles of rebellion, anger, alcoholism, drug use, sexually exploitative behaviors. Every fall I see students come and "stake out their territory" in the first few weeks of the year. They choose a group that is somewhere "on the edge." Now that they are on their own, they can reject the values that were so restrictive at home. But I also see those students in December and January and May. I see the pain and defeat that come from their choices. Sometimes I even see them as they leave school early or drop out because of their involvement with "lesser things."

The night before I left for college my high-school softball coach arranged a "spontaneous" visit. I just happened to be at home and not busy. It was a hot August night, so his suggestion that we go to Seven Dwarfs for ice cream sounded like a fine idea. I haven't forgotten his words. He told me that you only get one really good shot at college. He told me that many people start out and get mixed up in things that aren't worthy of their time, and he said, "Give it your best shot. Do it right the first time." Fight the good fight.

Finish the Race

When Paul was in Thessalonica, he asked the sisters and brothers there to pray that the message of the Lord might spread rapidly. A good paraphrase is "May the word of the Lord have a glorified run in us." What a picture to carry with you into the year: the Lord is running his race through you. In that metaphor we are the athletes running well or poorly, wearing the insignia of Christ, carrying his banner in the race.

My prayer for you is that you will finish the race. It is one thing to start. We have all started journeys many times in life. It is another thing altogether to finish.

One student I know did not. Shelly's early college life found her caught up in things she didn't really want. When she got away from home she found a new freedom to sneak off campus to "party at the U." Her drinking became a regular feature of her life. What she didn't realize is that alcohol lowers inhibitions and resistance—not only yours but others' too. She doesn't remember the night of her rape at all, not after the drinking started. But she woke up and she knew something precious had been taken from her. It hadn't started as a big deal—"I'm just going to the party to watch. I'm not going to drink." Then, "I'm just going to drink a little and go home. I'll keep things under control."

But she didn't, and it cost her plenty. What started out as the greatest opportunity of her life deteriorated quickly into a painful and degrading tragedy.

Will you finish the race? Researchers tell us that the first five to seven weeks of the semester or quarter are critical for the year. Who you choose to be, what you choose to do, where you choose to invest yourself in those weeks will shape much of the year for you. Many voices will demand your attention. Choose carefully and choose wisely.

Keep the Faith
In every age of church history some have abandoned a faith once begun. They have been unable or unwilling to pursue it to the end. I talked once to a college student friend who said, "I'm going back to school with one thing firmly in mind: I cannot keep the faith all by myself; I need the support and encouragement of other Christians. I tried to go it alone this summer and almost lost it altogether."

'Though Paul was threatened by his own vulnerability, he could declare with energy, "I have kept the faith." Don't misunderstand me. You may face times of uncertainty, confusion, even doubt. I am not urging you to a blind, uncritical obedience to some authority who wants to spoon-feed you and tell you everything to believe. If college life is doing its job well, it will create times of confusion in which you will be compelled to think about yourself and your faith—to consider and reconsider what it all means.

Over the past few years I have encountered many students who belong in a hall of fame for their courage and persistence. They have faced challenges from faculty who ridiculed their faith, from roommates whose lifestyles scorned the Christian faith, from parents whose values mocked the faith of the student. Many others have battled illnesses, defeats, disappointments and financial struggles just to stay in school. But they kept the faith. They kept the faith and hung in there because they discovered that they were not alone, that God was there to walk through the battle with them.

Brian was a powerful young man, an athlete, a football star in his own right. He came to college without a clear faith of his own, and he always hung around on the fringe of things. He tended to go whichever way the winds blew. Sometimes he was in and sometimes he was not. Brian needed to make up his mind. Practicing for the big game on Saturday was important. It got him ready. Getting on the team bus to head to the stadium was also a good idea. It carried him right to the arena. But until he got off the bus and stepped onto the field he was not in the game. He was still practicing. He never got to play.

One year I stood in a locker room with five senior football players. I drew a circle in the dust on the floor, and I laid out this challenge to them: "If you are ready to fight the good fight, throw your hat into the circle. If not, then you've made your choice." If they threw their hats into the circle, I told them I would expect them not only to start but to finish. I told them that I would be there to support them, but I would also push them, and sometimes push them hard, to keep the faith and to finish the course.

After a long, awkward silence the first man threw his hat in the circle, then the second, the third, the fourth and finally the fifth. What did it mean? They had made up their minds. They were ready to pick their fights.

Fight the good fight.
Finish the race.
Keep the faith.

Questions for Groups

1. Are you better as a starter or a finisher? Tell each other about times in your life when you started and didn't finish with the energy and satisfaction you had desired.

2. Talk about one "distraction" that you can identify that you have recognized in the early days of the year. How might this affect your ability to "finish the race"?

3. Identify your top priorities for the next four weeks of the school year. Be very practical—for example, "I plan to study four hours per day. I plan to find one mission or service opportunity in the next four weeks. I plan to spend thirty minutes a day in prayer and Bible study."

4. Ask each other: How can we pray for you in the week ahead?

4

Choose Your Own Adventure

One thing you discover almost instantly is that college life gives you great new freedom. Your mother or father isn't standing over you now to tell you when to get up, when to come in at night, when to study, when to wash your clothes and what to eat.

Jeff came to campus certain of one important thing: he was free. His parents were four hundred miles away, and he could do as he pleased. He started the year living according to his own rules, ignoring the college's rules and his parents' values. He ignored the warnings and disciplinary actions in his dorm and on campus until finally in December he discovered that his freedom made him free for only one thing, to leave college and sit out for a year. The misuse of his freedom took away what he wanted most.

The New Testament book of Galatians has something important to say about freedom, although it's a puzzling paradox. Paul says that freedom is expressed in accountability. While some people think that freedom and accountability are contradictions, the Bible disagrees. It says that freedom is authentic only under the restraint of accountability. Paul says, "For you were called to freedom, brothers and sisters; only do not use your freedom as an opportunity for self-indulgence, but through love become slaves to one another. For the whole law is summed up in a single commandment, 'You shall love your neighbor as yourself' " (Gal 5:13-14).

Big Enough for Freedom

Freedom recognizes that we are interrelated, and thus accountable to one another. It recognizes that we do not live as lone rangers, but that we are interconnected to one another. My freedom is not absolute, but has a built-in accountability to others.

Once I made a kite. I cut the wood, fit the paper onto that fragile frame and attached a long roll of string. I learned how to keep it going and let it fly farther and farther away each time. I learned how to regulate the length of the tail so it could fly higher and higher. I flew that kite at fantastic heights and let it soar and sail in the wind, but I always kept the tail in sight.

One fateful day in South Park, however, as the kite soared into the heights, it seemed to say, "Wow, is it beautiful up here. Flying in this breeze, I can see the world. If it weren't for this string I could fly forever. I could travel and not be limited by this string. If only I could get this string to let me go, I would truly become free." And so it gathered all its kitely strength together and pulled and pulled until finally the string gave way and the kite was lifted by the air currents to even greater heights—but only for a moment; and then it began to dive ever so quickly. The inevitable crash landing came only seconds later, and the beautiful "Hy-Flyer" from W. T. Grants and Co. was demolished. What the kite didn't realize was that it needed the force of that string to provide a tension against the wind to give it freedom to fly. Without the restraint of that string, the wind became an enemy, and the freedom discovered in the string was lost. Without a string, the kite wasn't free at all.

"Do not use your freedom as an opportunity for self-indulgence, but through love become slaves to one another." Why? Because true freedom is expressed in accountability. The opportunity to serve one another is like that kite. Accountability keeps our freedom in flight. Few biblical teachings cut across the grain of our self-indulgent culture more than this one. Our culture touts our freedom to do anything we choose, but if you look again you will see a culture of selfish individualism gone rampant. A guest from Uganda said recently that Americans love their freedom, but their freedom often leads them into slavery.

That is true, perhaps because freedom is often determined by what I am free *not* to do. Paul writes in 1 Corinthians, " 'All things are lawful for me,' but not all things are beneficial. 'All things are lawful for me,' but I will not be dominated by anything" (6:12). I may be free, but authentic freedom demands of me that I also be accountable.

A foreign exchange student from Europe came to the United States to study. After her year was up, she was asked if she would like to remain in America. In her words, "America is indeed a wonderful land in which to live. I should like the advantages of your way of living, but I'm afraid I'm not a big enough person to live in such freedom." Big enough for freedom. Perhaps she saw more deeply than we do that to live in freedom is also to live in accountability.

I may be free to do anything, but accountability demands that I be big enough to know when to stop or when not to exercise all of my freedom. As a well-fed American, I may be free to eat to excess without a twinge of conscience, but accountability demands that I consume my food with the hunger of the Third World in mind. As a consumer with many things in my home, I may be free to purchase more and more, but accountability demands that I allow the values of Jesus Christ to fill my wants, that I may share my resources with others. I may be free to have all kinds of sexual experiences, but accountability reminds me to think carefully before I do. I need to remember that God expects us to treat each other as subjects, not objects, and that completely free, casual sex is a step toward bondage. I may be free to insulate myself and turn my back on the needs of the poor, but accountability demands that I make my decisions, economically and politically, with the needs of the poor in mind.

In *Rare Beasts, Unique Adventures: Reflections for College Students,* Linda Lawrence says,

> From the moment you step on the campus, your heart will be pulled to many allegiances, each clamoring for your loyalty, each parading the promises of the good life. . . . What is so confusing is that each of these has positive values and is worthy of effort. But are they worthy of our trust? Are they worth centering our lives on? . . . The call to love God with all our heart is not just a belief in an abstract

idea, nor a demand, but a dazzling invitation to enter into a relationship with a living God.

When my own children were small, one of their favorite pastimes was reading. As they became college students, reading became more like a vocation than an avocation, but I remember when reading was purely for fun. Kevin's favorite books were a series called Choose Your Own Adventure. In these books you read along in the story until you come to a critical juncture, where you personally decide what course of action the major character—you—will take. The cover of *Escape* sets the stage: "You're the star of the story! Choose from the twenty-seven possible endings." The year is 2035. You are in enemy territory. Your job is to fly the Doradan invasion plans to Turtalian headquarters. You have almost completed your mission when you come face to face with enemy patrol planes. What happens next in the story? It all depends on the choices you make.

Like these books, the choices you freely make today have implications for the steps you will take tomorrow. The worst decision is to allow others to choose for you. This means losing your freedom.

One of my heroes today is Wayne Gordon. About seventeen years ago this white Iowa boy chose the adventure of teaching in a predominantly African-American inner-city high school. Not only that, he began to invite kids to his home and eventually bought a duplex so the kids could hang out in one of the apartments. From that has come a ministry in the fifteenth-poorest neighborhood in the United States and an adventure that "Coach" would never trade for anything. When he speaks about his life's work, his eyes glow with an excitement that I see only in the eyes of those who have made "kingdom choices" with their lives. He has chosen to use his freedom for a larger good. He chose the adventure!

The Best Is Still Ahead

One writer has said, "It is dangerous to have one's golden age behind one. It is the opposite of adventure. . . . For the child, the golden age is always now and is always yet to come." Some studies today show a pervading pessimism among the current generation. One asked people aged fifteen to twenty-four: "Are America's best years ahead of us or behind?" Only 37 percent answered that the best years are still ahead. A majority, 54 percent, answered "Behind us" (W. Strauss and N. Howe, *13th Generation: Abort, Retry, Ignore, Fail?*). More than half believed it is all over already. The party was last decade, and we missed it! Well, I don't buy those statistics. I am not ready to give up on an entire generation, especially Christian college students. I look at the future through the lens of the kingdom of God and see a vision of God empowering an entire generation of students to bring serious change to the world.

At the same time that people lament the apathy and cynicism of this generation, statistics show that the number of freshmen listing "participating in community action programs" as one of their goals reached its highest level in a decade in 1992 (A. W. Astin, W. S. Korn and E. R. Riggs, *The American Freshman: National Norms for Fall 1993*). I see a new wave of activism in outreach and missions programs on Christian college campuses. I see the excitement and readiness in the eyes of students who want to be part of what's happening in ministries to children, young people, the poor, the elderly, the oppressed. I see interest in international missions on the rise and a strong desire for hands-on involvement in things that matter.

My friend Chad went to Chicago with me one May. We just happened to spend some time at Wrigley Field, home of my favorite baseball team, the Chicago Cubs. After the game, Chad took off to see the city. He met some homeless men on the street who asked him for money. He asked them what they would do with the money if he gave it to them—would they buy wine? They told him the truth and said yes. He refused to do that, but instead invited them to join him for pizza. It was a risk, maybe even a foolish thing to do, but before that pizza was eaten, those men had heard about Chad's best friend, Jesus Christ. Chad's sense of the adventure of the kingdom of God greatly increased because he took a risk with his faith. I saw him again not too long ago, and he's still in the business of taking risks with his faith. He finds life to be a constantly unfolding adventure. What about you?

You are a generation that can ignite the fire of the church. You are a generation that can launch a movement of spiritual fire and change that can sweep the American church and bring it into a new reformation. You are a generation that can lead the church into the future of God's intentions.

Questions for Groups

1. Can you identify one of your childhood heroes? Why was this person a hero to you then? Is that person still a hero for you? Why or why not?
2. Has anything adventuresome happened for you since you prayed for an adventuresome faith in your last meeting?
3. What has been the greatest thing about your freedom in your life as a college or university student? What has been the most surprising or toughest thing?
4. Pray for a wise use of freedom for each group member.

5

Friends Are Forever?
Give Me a Break!

Early in the first chapter of *The Adventures of Huckleberry Finn* we read:

> Then they all stuck a pin in their fingers to get blood to sign with, and I made my mark on the paper.
>
> "Now," says Ben Rogers, "what's the line of business of this Gang?"
>
> "Nothing, only robbery and murder," Tom said.

Thus began a friendship that took those boys all up and down the mighty Mississippi River into every sort of adventure imaginable. Many of us also sealed childhood friendships that way. With the bond of blood between us we became "blood brothers to one another" and took an oath of friendship forever. We gave our solemn word of loyalty.

I recently took an informal survey of college catalogs. For a while I thought that the same four people traveled as photographic models for colleges across the nation, because every catalog showed a group of people doing what you do most in college: hanging out and being friends. Every catalog seems to send the same message: come to college and make lifelong friends. I hope that's true, but I also think that, unfortunately, far too many of us have never grown up into a more adult understanding of friendship.

I once stood behind a group of students at the close of a retreat, listening to them sing Michael W. Smith's song "Friends Are Friends Forever"—and heard the cynical reply of one student, "Friends are friends forever? Give me a break!"

At least he understood that friendship is not the sentimental experience portrayed by Mark Twain. It is a complex and fragile process. In our drive-through, fast-food society, we are pretty good at superficial relationships, but true friendships are hard to come by.

Dan told me recently that his friend Pete is "a friend for life, closer than a brother, someone whom I trust with everything." What builds such friendships? The lives of Jonathan and David as described in the Old Testament offer a window into that kind of friendship.

How to Be a Good Friend
The first quality of friendship is that it is an investment of one's self in another. In Jonathan we see a willingness to invest himself in David. He made the first move, attempting to relax any worries that David might have had about the social gap between them. After all, one was the prince and one was the servant of the king. As a sign of the covenant between them, "Jonathan stripped himself of the robe that he was wearing, and gave it to David, and his armor, and even his sword and his bow and his belt" (1 Sam 18:4). An exchange of weapons like this was an ancient way of sealing a friendship.

This willingness to invest oneself in another is of crucial importance in any friendship. You cannot guarantee that another person will be your friend; you cannot seek them out that they may love you. That's the surest way to miss your goal. But imitating Jonathan will give certain results. He gave all of the symbols of his royalty to David. He invested himself freely in his friend. The question we have to ask is not, "How can I go out and find a Jonathan for my life?" but rather, "To whom am I a Jonathan?" The question is, "What kind of friend am I?"

C. S. Lewis has a wonderful statement about friendship in *The Four Loves:*

> For the Christian there are, strictly speaking, no chances. A secret master of ceremonies has already been at work. The same Lord who said to his disciples, "You have not chosen me but I have chosen you," says to every group of Christian friends, "You have not chosen each other, but I have chosen you for each other." And the friend-

ship is not a reward for our discrimination and taste in seeking one another out. It is the instrument by which God reveals to each the beauties of all the others.

A second quality of friendship is that it is a *committed* investment of one's self in another. You have neither the time nor the energy to love every person you meet. Genuine, deep friendship is possible only with a few specific people.

M. Scott Peck writes in *The Road Less Traveled* that "love is not simply giving; it is *judicious* giving and judicious withholding as well." If you are to be friends, you will have to make certain choices about those friendships. You cannot be there for everyone, or you will burn out. There just isn't enough to go around.

After David became Saul's servant and consequently a high-ranking military official, a rift began to develop between them. Jealousy brewed within Saul until he set out to kill David. But Jonathan chose to stand against his father. He stood beside David, taking his part, taking his side against the king. He even warned David of Saul's plot to kill him and spoke for David to the king.

Friendship involves choices that require action. When you love someone, you are willing to exert yourself for them. You choose to love them, sometimes despite the hardship that choice might create. Declarations of friendship are not enough. Friendship is more than the passing of years. It is more than the shallow superficialities one too often experiences. Friendship is a *committed* investment of one's self in another.

Third, friendship is a *vulnerable* committed investment of one's self in another. Eventually Jonathan saw that his father's threats on David's life were so serious that David had to leave. He arranged David's escape, and they met for one last time before they had to separate. In their final meeting they expressed their deep emotion, affection and trust in a covenant to protect each other and their children (1 Sam 20).

Friendship is a *vulnerable* relationship. There is no such thing as friendship without risk—of loss, rejection or betrayal. Friendship requires risk and demands a price.

Five guys met weekly because they were told it was "good for your spiritual growth." In fact, they did it because they laughed a lot together and enjoyed each other's company. In time, however, they moved to a new stage in their relationships and began to trust each other enough to get vulnerable. One night Gary said, "Sometime I'll tell you the truth about me." A few weeks later he did. He told them about his high-school girlfriend and their sexual activity. He confessed this to his friends and said, "I guess you'll want me to quit the group, now that you know the truth about me." After a long moment of silence a grin cracked on someone's face. It grew into a smile and finally into laughter—loud and free laughter, not the laughter of judgment but of grace given. Gary was only the first to tell his story and risk being vulnerable.

Finally, friendship is a *mutual,* vulnerable, committed investment of one's self in another. Jonathan and David spoke the truth together, each one giving and taking. Jonathan agreed to sound out the king about David, but then he asked something of David. It is a poignant moment in their lives. Jonathan knew that David was God's choice to be king: "If I am still alive, show me the faithful love of the Lord; but if I die, never cut off your faithful love from my house, even if the Lord were to cut off every one of the enemies of David from the face of the earth" (1 Sam 20:14-15).

Friendship requires that kind of *mutuality.* A one-sided relationship is an unhealthy dependence and not a truly authentic friendship. You must be willing to give and to receive. Jonathan and David's friendship had progressed to the point that they each wanted the best for the other. And what they wanted most for the other was God's best in the other's life. That is the ultimate goal of any friendship in Christ: to seek God's best for each other's life. There is a secret in all of this found in Jonathan's name. His name in Hebrew is derived from *Yah*—the Lord and *natan*—gives. The Lord gives.

David and Jonathan were friends. But more, their friendship is a model of true friendship, showing God's intention that we grow up in our friendships. The choice is before you.

Questions for Groups
1. Who was your best friend as a child?

What made that person so important to you?

2. Who is your closest friend now?

What makes that person so important to you?

3. What has changed between childhood and now? What do you need from adult friendships that was not present in childhood?

4. Pray for each person in the group by name. Ask each person to tell you the most pressing need they have today.

6

This Is *My* Room: Rippin' on Roommates

One of the most exciting—and scary—parts of adjusting to college life is meeting and living with a complete stranger. After a few short weeks you may have a new best friend—or worst enemy. Understandably, roommate problems exist. The college puts two strangers into a twelve-by-twelve-foot room with matching beds, dressers and desks and says to them: "Become best friends." You don't know each other, your values and tastes may be completely different, you may listen to totally different kinds of music—and yet somehow you're to get along and even become lifelong friends. Some people in residence life simply hope they'll get through a semester together without burning down the dorm.

The struggles may be many and can take different forms. Some students have never had to share a room with anyone before, so the concept is new to them. Others are used to sharing rooms—and everything else—with a brother or a sister. In every case, adjustments to dorm living are necessary.

What are some guidelines or suggestions for making this roommate thing work? The answer is the same as in any other significant relationship: respect, communication and adapting.

Respect can start even before you get to campus. Begin by evaluating your expectations for your roommate. You must realize that it will be different from having a room to yourself. It will be different from living

Top Ten Roommate Complaints

Some of the common roommate problems are not a surprise to anyone who's lived in a dorm. This list was culled from a conversation with about twenty-five resident assistants.

1. Lack of respect for each other's space.
2. "He likes rap; I like Amy Grant."
3. "She borrows my _____" [money, car keys, deodorant—I hope not toothbrushes].
4. "I'm up at 7:00 a.m., he sleeps until noon."
5. "I plan my studying ahead. She pulls all-nighters every week."
6. The abandoned roommate syndrome: "We used to be best friends until she got a boyfriend." Sometimes dating jealousy turns into a self-esteem battle. "I'm so ugly, no one wants to date me."
7. "I'm a slob, but he lives in a garbage dump."
8. "I'm an introvert; she's a social butterfly."
9. "I study, he plays hockey. I enjoy listening to chapel talks; he brings his radio. I'm involved in many campus activities; she goes home every weekend. I'm growing in my faith; she doesn't even own a Bible. I'm part of the outreach movement on campus; he comes home drunk three nights a week."
10. The inconsiderate roommate: "She listens to loud music when I'm trying to sleep."

at home. Your musical tastes may be different. You may be neat and he may use the "drop and kick" method of storing his clothes. You may study early and she may not start until midnight. Think hard about what you really expect it to be like.

Check your baggage at the door when you arrive. Open yourself up for the unique experience of living with a new person. Create your own expectations and guidelines together. Many residence hall arrangements place you with four or even six people. Some students find it helpful to create a "covenant" that outlines the basic "rules of the house." Start with a basic attitude of respect for your roommate's space, time and possessions. Remember that this is *shared* space. The attitude that says, "Hey, this is *my* room," forgets that this is also *our* room. Early in the year, set clear boundaries for use of each other's things.

Avoid the "nickel and dime" cycle. Dave told me that his roommate was always borrowing—quarters for laundry, a couple of cans of soft drink, the last of the chips, just a cup of laundry soap, and so forth. In frustration Dave responded in kind by becoming an accountant. Every time his roommate borrowed—with or without asking—he wrote it down in a ledger and began to "charge" his roommate for a slice of pizza or a cup of soap. Needless to say, they parted ways, and not as best friends.

Communicate regularly with your roommate. Take time to get to know each other, to support and challenge each other. Pray together on a regular basis. It may not be every day, but make some time to listen to each other and to pray for each other.

Mountain climbers do something called a shakedown about half an hour out on the climb. They stop and check things out, adjusting packs and readjusting loads if necessary. They check to see if their boots are snug and if their outer clothing is suited to their body temperature and to the weather. They do it soon after starting so that they can make any necessary adjustments. There is nothing worse than the irritating rub of a wool sock on a blister or a pack that begins to rub on a shoulder. What starts out as a minor irritant may expand into a major problem that might stop you from continuing on the climb. Schedule time for regular "shakedowns" with your roommate.

If you have a conflict or disagreement, cool down and think about it before you put on the boxing gloves for ten rounds. Honesty in love is what Paul urges. Tell the truth—no holds barred—but do it in love. How you tell your roommate about the problem will matter. If you end every sentence with a phrase like "you jerk," then you're probably not going to resolve this conflict soon.

Avoid the triangle. On many campuses the communication system works like this—I am mad at you, so I talk to someone else. (I may even use the gossip-disguised-as-prayer-request technique: I tell you, but only so you can pray for her). Talk to your roommate first. Don't tell your fifty closest friends first, because one of them will distort the message and get the word to your roommate anyway (so *she* can pray about it). Don't "rip" on your roommate to other people; take it to the roommate first.

Avoid the "sticky note system." I actually heard about a student who left sticky notes for his roommate rather than talk it out face to face. They said things like "I'm in bed, you should be too." "I cleaned up my side of the room. It's your turn to sweep all the dust and crud from under your filthy side of the room." Talking it over may be harder, but the results will be better.

Remember that no problem is 100 percent the other person's. If the conflict escalates, seek out help. Resident assistants and the residence hall director are there to mediate.

Forgiveness is essential. Where there are conflicts and disagreements, keep short accounts. Paul said, "Don't let the sun go down on your anger," which means "finish today's conflicts today and don't brood over them." Don't carry over old baggage from this quarter into next quarter or this semester into next year. Finish your business with each other before you head home for the summer.

A good way to avoid conflict is to learn to adapt. Pay attention to how your behavior affects your roommate. Be willing to use earphones or to study elsewhere if your sleep schedules conflict. Give a little, and then give a little more. Flexibility will go a long way. Without flexibility and compromise no relationship will survive.

If you're in a dating relationship, remember that the room still belongs to your roommate too. Don't bring your boyfriend or girlfriend around so often that your roommate loses his or her privacy.

Keep your sense of humor about you, and learn to relax. Don't sweat the small stuff.

Set realistic hopes and expectations for your roommate. Don't expect your roommate to be your best friend for life. If that happens, as it sometimes does, it is a great gift. If not, you can develop a workable relationship and learn a great deal from the experience.

And finally, keep at it. Talk it over before you need to say, "I want out!" You may be tempted to quit and throw in the towel, but keep at it.

Questions for Groups

1. Create your own top ten list of roommate complaints that you have heard about.

2. Create another top ten list of tips you would give to someone about to have a roommate for the first time.

3. Sit down with your own roommate and ask if any of these problems exist in your room.

4. Pray for your roommate, your floor, your residence hall.

7

Holy Ground

One day a young female student stopped by the office of a faculty friend of mine to discuss some matters of academic importance (like why she didn't get an A on her last exam). All during the conversation she stared at him. In fact, she began to stare deep into his eyes, and this middle-aged professor began to say things to himself like: *Well, maybe you still have what it takes to be attractive to young women. Maybe the old looks haven't left you after all.* She stared and stared, looking deeper and deeper into his eyes. All the time he delivered an eloquent discourse on some esoteric academic subject because he just knew she was enraptured by his wit and wisdom. Finally, she spoke. "Professor, those are the dirtiest glasses I have ever seen in my entire life. How can you see out of them?"

Sometimes it's hard to pay attention! However, the essence of spirituality has to do with attention—paying attention to the presence of God in our lives. It's an energizing way to live—alive, alert and ready to hear.

I teach a class on urban studies in Chicago every year. We often start the course with a challenge from Andrew Greeley, who invites people to see "God lurking everywhere in the city." We look for God on every street corner, in every alley, train station and bus.

An old Russian proverb says, "Every day is a messenger of God." Every day will bring many voices into your hearing, voices that will demand your attention. This means that one of the most important things to practice is learning to hear God speak in the routines of your life.

Practicing the Presence of God

Brother Lawrence was a cook in a monastery. He learned to discover meaning in virtually everything he did. It is said that he learned to peel potatoes and cook food to the glory of God, always "practicing the presence of God" in every activity. He understood that life is sacred in all of its parts, not merely when we are in church or in a worship experience or doing something "religious." His writings are captured in a wonderful little book, *Practicing the Presence of God*. Listen to what he said:

> Lift up your heart to Him, sometimes even at your meals, and when you are in company; the least little remembrance will always be acceptable to Him. You need not cry very loud; He is nearer to us than we know.
>
> It is not necessary for being with God to be always at church. We may make an oratory of our heart wherein to retire from time to time to converse with Him in meekness, humility, and love. Everyone is capable of such familiar conversation with God, some more, some less. He knows what we can do. Let us begin, then.

Brother Lawrence's goal in life was to do everything for the love of God, to make use of all the tasks in his life in awareness of God's presence. His message rings true with its simplicity: we can learn to practice the presence of God.

I recently received a letter from a former student, telling me about her experiences in beginning graduate school. She wrote:

> I am enjoying this new season of my life. It is of course difficult to leave friends, but I am gradually getting to know people. Much of my joy comes from the glimpses of God that I see nearly daily. Seriously, Keith, I truly believe that God is intervening in my history to calm me and assure me of His presence as I take new and unfamiliar steps.

Paying attention for glimpses of God. What an image to carry with you!

The book of Genesis tells the story of Jacob's escape from his brother Esau. One night, near the city of Luz, he had a dream in which he envisioned what has become known as "Jacob's ladder," a staircase leading into the heavens. God spoke to him in his dream and blessed him and his offspring. Jacob awoke and said, "How awesome is this place! This is none other than the house of God, and this is the gate of heaven." In the morning, Jacob built an altar and renamed the place *Beth-el.* Thus Luz, an unimportant, out-of-the-way place, became Bethel, the house of God. What was once a common place, a place of failure, a place of confusion, became a sacred place because Jacob chose to open his eyes and see the holiness of the moment. He looked, he listened, he paid attention. He said, "Surely the Lord is in this place— and I did not know it!"

Take Off Your Shoes

A couple of years ago, while reading the book of Exodus, I became fascinated by an encounter Moses had with God.

> Moses was keeping the flock of his father-in-law Jethro, the priest of Midian; he led his flock beyond the wilderness, and came to Horeb, the mountain of God. There the angel of the Lord appeared to him in a flame of fire out of a bush; he looked, and the bush was blazing, yet it was not consumed. Then Moses said, "I must turn aside and look at this great sight, and see why the bush is not burned up." When the Lord saw that he had turned aside to see, God called to him out of the bush, "Moses, Moses!" And he said, "Here I am." Then he said, "Come no closer! Remove the sandals from your feet, for the place on which you are standing is holy ground." (Ex 3:1-5)

I have often used this text to call people to become alert to everything surrounding them. It reminds us to become awakened to God's voice in common things around us. It reminds us that anything can become a container for sacred things, for holy things. It reminds us to pay attention because God may be lurking anywhere. I said that one day and a student took offense, telling me that God doesn't "lurk." I disagree, because, like many others, I have been surprised and "ambushed" by God, who showed up at times when I didn't expect him. I have learned from Moses that even the very soil on which we stand can become sacred ground, holy ground, a consecrated place.

Many students discover a great resource for life during the college years. Some call it the daily quiet time or the devotional life or something very spiritual-sounding. One could also simply call it time out to pay attention. Time out to read God's Word and listen. Time out to pray to God and to listen. Time out to reflect and think and to listen. How long should this time be? What are the "right" steps to take? When should it be done—morning, afternoon or evening? These details vary

---

RPMs for Spiritual Power

While there is no single way to pay attention to God, three basic requirements are most important. You should find your own way to use them. I call them the RPM method for spiritual power:

☐ Read Scripture—but remember to do so not only to gain information but also to meet Jesus.

☐ Pray—but remember that in prayer you spend time with Jesus, whom you meet in the Word.

☐ Meditate—but remember, your goal is to love Jesus with your heart and mind.

Find the time, the place and the system that work best for you.

---

from person to person, but the need is common to us all. When we say, like Moses, "I must turn aside and see this great sight," we hear the voice of God calling us by name and saying, "Remove the sandals from your feet, for the place on which you are standing is holy ground."

One of my students asked me how to pay attention. "Daily devotions doesn't always work for me like I've been told it should," she said.

"What's the biblical way to do devotions?" I asked, tongue-in-cheek.

"Well, I don't think there is one biblical way, is there?" she replied.

"No," I agreed. "I think there's Moses' way and David's way and Paul's way and Hannah's way and Mary's way."

Each of these people seem to have had their own way of listening to

God. God has created us with uniqueness. Perhaps the way we pay attention to God is also somewhat unique. Some students pray best alone in a quiet room; others find it easier to pay attention with music playing and with a group of others around.

This may be the easiest chapter of all to remember. The message is simple: pay attention!

Questions for Groups
1. When have you stopped to listen this week?
What did you hear?
2. What's the hardest part about listening?
3. Identify one time when you will intentionally take time out to listen to God in the next week.
4. Pray that each group member will learn the discipline of waiting before God in prayerful listing.

8

Legos and
Worldviews

I received a letter from a student who said, "Keith, I want you to know, I will continue to ask my questions and to ask them boldly. Thanks for helping me learn to believe in myself." That is a formula for an exciting life of growth! If your education is working you will be forced into some times of searching, of asking questions.

When Minh was in high school, his youth pastor told him that he needed to submit to the pastor's authority. Translated that meant, "Don't ask questions. I'll give you the answers."

On the contrary, your questions are invaluable. If you never ask the questions, of what value are the answers? If you only ask other people's questions, where is *your* faith? If you never ask about the great mysteries, who is doing your thinking for you? I firmly believe that the college years are the right time to begin to explore, to search, to wrestle with issues and questions.

I think Paul agrees. In Romans 12:1-2 he talks about building a worldview.

> I appeal to you therefore, brothers and sisters, by the mercies of God, to present your bodies as a living sacrifice, holy and acceptable to God, which is your spiritual worship. Do not be conformed to this world, but be transformed by the renewing of your minds, so that you may discern what is the will of God—what is good and acceptable and perfect.

Paul is talking about the use of your mind, even the use of your questions. He tells us something we need to think about if we are to grow. To begin with, we cannot do it alone. "I appeal to you therefore, brothers and sisters." Notice that the words are directed to the community first of all.

This is a huge truth: Students who grow seldom grow in isolation from one another. They need connections with other Christians. Lone ranger Christians can dazzle themselves and others for a while, but they will not stand up in the long run.

An old African proverb says, "Because we are, I am—I am because we are." Because of the community of home and family and history, I am. Because we as community exist, I am. Because of my connections with others, I am. Without the help of the community, I will not be strong, I will not exist as I am now. Another African proverb that has become more widely known states, "It takes a village to raise a child." We don't arrive at maturity all by ourselves. And we don't build faith alone. We need one another.

Paul also tells us to be careful not to conform, to let the world around us squeeze us into its mold. Instead, he says, "be transformed by the renewing of your minds." Don't let the group decide for you who you're going to be or what values will become your values. That's a hard road to travel for many of us. Because we need the acceptance and validation of others, we are sometimes too willing to become what the group decides. We soon let the group become the ones who define our values for us. Many students find themselves experimenting with many new (and sometimes illegal) activities simply because the group has decided for them. Paul warns us against such conformity and calls us to be transformed or changed or converted by renewing our minds. Don't let someone else do your thinking for you!

Questions, Questions, Questions

Will Rogers said, "I believe in college because it gets the young person out of the house just as he begins to ask the really hard questions." If he is right, then your parents happily sent you to college hoping that the school would work through those hard questions with you. He's right about one thing: College is the right time for thinking. It's the right time for you to think and to choose values that are your own. Start with your own questions. Ask your questions of those with wisdom and insight to answer them carefully.

A couple of years ago a student stood in the doorway of my office to complain about a chapel message. "I don't think I agree with you," she said. We talked for about twenty minutes. A week later she was back with a similar complaint about the sermon. After a while I figured out that she was testing me, checking me out to see how I would handle her bold questions and concerns. As time progressed, she trusted me with more of her questions, and we're still working on them. Some of her questions don't have answers—they require someone to live them. Not surprisingly, when she chose a major it was theology. The focus for her ongoing studies became clear because she was free to pursue her questions. What questions motivate you to think and to act?

Some of you have the benefit of attending a college where your faculty are Christians who will challenge you but still support you in your faith. That's not true for everyone. Others face a great battle for the mind in classrooms where secularism and relativism rule the day. The mistake in either case is to run and hide from the questions. Remember, we need each other to help us think *faith*fully. In every situation you need to find a community of Christians who will help you

---

Worldview Reading

What building blocks will you choose in building your worldview? Will you look to the front page of *The Wall Street Journal*? Will you turn on Channel 9 or MTV? Will you tune in CNN, or will you pick up a popular magazine? Will you follow the cues of *Baywatch*, the soaps or *Roseanne*? Will you discuss it with your roommates and come to a group consensus?

Books by Christian thinkers will help you to answer the hard questions in life as you develop a Christian worldview. Look for books by James Sire, Arthur Holmes, Tony Campolo, Tom Sine, Brennan Manning, Jill Briscoe and Gordon MacDonald.

to ask the questions honestly and to build a biblical worldview.

We All Play with Building Blocks

You know what Legos are—plastic building blocks that snap together into designs that you create. They are a toy, but they are also an opportunity for the child to build, to construct, to create. In fact, after they were already named, someone discovered that in Latin *lego* means "I build" or "I construct." Many of you will admit that somewhere in your closet at home is a box that contains some of these wonderful toys. They are an excellent toy because they require creativity from the person using them. I've been thinking about them because they remind me of what higher education is all about.

One of the primary goals for Christian higher education is to facilitate the construction of a worldview. A worldview is the picture of reality that you carry in your head. In *The Universe Next Door,* James Sire defines *worldview* as assumptions or presuppositions about the basic makeup of the world. What is real? What is the world really like? Is this a safe place, a scary place, a friendly place or an evil and cruel place? Whoever we are, we all build a worldview, an image of how the world is, and we carry it with us consciously or unconsciously.

Life provides us all with a set of building blocks and allows us to create our own worldview. That worldview may work for us and provide deep meaning, or it may collapse like a badly constructed Lego creation. It may provide stability, strength and a solid foundation for life, or it may break apart and crumble.

Some years ago I was called to the hospital in the middle of the night. Shirley was dying. I was told to hurry if I wanted to see her before she died. I made it there only moments before she breathed her last breath. I was glad for a conversation we had had a few weeks before. She had grabbed my hand one afternoon as I visited her in the hospital. "Keith, it's time for truth," she said. "We both know I'm going to die very soon. The cancer has spread into so many parts of my body, we know it can't be long. But I need to know, how can I be sure I'll be OK after I die? What do I need to do to make sure everything will be OK on the other side of this life?"

Where do you look for an answer to a question like that? Your worldview will determine that for you. I don't know about you, but I wanted the next words out of my mouth to have more authority than the logic I could muster on my own.

A. E. Levine reports in the journal *Change* that researchers have found that five events have most influenced this generation: the *Challenger* explosion, the end of the Cold War, the Persian Gulf War, AIDS and the beating of Rodney King. Your worldview helps you to interpret and make sense out of major influential events like these.

Paul tells us that the basis for a Christian worldview is Jesus—none other than the One in whom the very fullness of God dwells. In Jesus you are given access to the fullness of God, the mind of God, the heart of God, the Spirit of God. What does that mean? It means that you are not left on your own to sort out all the philosophies of life. Rather, you have a trustworthy authority. As you get to know the mind of Christ you can make sense out of events like those listed above. As you understand Jesus' way of seeing the world, you can build a Christlike worldview that is big enough to face the crises and challenges that will come your way. Jesus Christ is the way through the maze of questions to a worldview that is rock-solid.

But, just like those Legos, your worldview is not a completed product, preconstructed in advance. You are given building blocks. You are not given a set of instructions that show in detail the steps needed to build your worldview. What you find instead is a relationship with One who has done some worldview building before, no less than a carpenter whose name is Jesus! Through that relationship, you learn how to use the building blocks of your life to create your worldview with a solid foundation. In that relationship you can ask all of your questions and pursue truth fearlessly, because you are not left alone to make sense out of the many options that exist. The Bible provides markers and signs that point in the right direction. Through a relationship with Jesus Christ, you can find the way and build a worldview that can face the very worst that life brings.

Questions for Groups

1. Did you ever play with Legos as a child? What was the greatest thing

you ever built with them or with other building toys?

2. What have you read or viewed this week that has contributed positively to the development of a Christian worldview for you? What have you read or viewed this week that has contributed negatively to the development of your Christian worldview?

3. Create a list of top ten questions you hope to find answers to in the year ahead.

4. Ask how you can pray for each other in the week ahead.

9

How Do You Spell Success?

Christa and I had talked many times. She asked questions and brought me topics so I could ask her questions. But this particular morning, she was agitated. "I have to know," she said. "I have to know what success is."

This question—Am I successful?—is a wonderful and a terrible question all at the same time. I hope you will ask it many times during your life as a college student. Most importantly, it is a question of definition: How do you define success? How will you know if you are successful when you get to wherever you're heading with your college work and your life after graduation?

The assumption is that the basis for success is clear to everyone: the three *m*'s—money, money, money. If I have money, then I must be successful; if I don't, then either I'm a college student en route to that target or I am not successful. But you must set your own criteria for success.

How Do You Spell Success?
One way you can measure success is by *who you are*. In his writings, Paul proudly lists reasons for confidence in who he is. One by one he enumerates the things that could give a sense of adequacy and importance and accomplishment. He says, "I am a Hebrew of the Hebrews . . . a law-obedient Jew, from the pure line, out of a special tribe" (Phil

3:5). These were his credentials and his credits. "I am somebody because of who I am."

Our culture measures success, at least partially, by these kinds of external standards. You are *somebody* if you come from the right neighborhood or schools or if you have the right background. You are successful and important if you look successful and important, which is measured by the car you drive, the cellular phone, the designer clothes and the right "look." The problem is that not everyone is a superstar; thus many would receive very low grades if success were measured by who we are.

In the world of college students beauty and attractiveness are often the measure of one's value. If you were given a perfect size-seven body with a beautiful face, great complexion and stunning eyes, then you are considered to be a person of worth. If you have the body of a professional athlete with a perfectly developed physique and a handsome face, then you are considered to be a person of worth. If you are popular, dated by many or even by one, then you are also considered to be a person of worth. But there is a great danger in buying into the *Sports Illustrated* swimsuit mentality. The danger is in substituting image or form for substance—trading in the substance of character and depth and spirituality for an external image.

Students are big on image. You can send certain signals simply by what you wear. Just as the gangs in our cities tip each other off by their colors, the tilt of their hat, their scarf or their hand signal, you too send subtle messages by the clothes you wear or by the style of your hair, by your shoes or coats. You may be J. Crew or you may be GQ. You may go with the jock style or wear army boots and purple hair! What you wear is, in part, a signal to others about you. You signal those with whom you want to hang out and those you choose not to notice. You signal those who are cool and those who are not. You even signal the way you see yourself.

Pastor James "Bo" Ford from the south side of Chicago says that we take credit for four things that we have no control over: race, face, place and grace. I think he's absolutely correct. They are ours because we have been given them by the hand of God. What did you do to choose your race, your face or your place? What did you do that brings you God's grace? The answer is simple: nothing! Why then do we treat them as if they were our accomplishment?

A second common yardstick for measuring success is *what you do*, and here again Paul has a long list. He says, in essence, "You need to understand that I was a Pharisee of the Pharisees. I grew up in a good religious home, but later on I realized for myself what Judaism was, and then I outdid even my own parents. I performed better than anybody. I became the best Pharisee there ever was. I followed the lifestyle of Israel to the fullest extent." These were Paul's assets. He not only *was* somebody, but he *did* something with his life. He was a success in who he was and even more in what he did.

You are no different. You take pride in what you do, which is fine when it's appropriate. It is good to be affirmed in one's work and for excellence in that work. But is performance an accurate measurement of success? How do you evaluate performance—by how much money you make? how much status you have? how much power and authority you exert? Nothing is inherently wrong with any of these: money, status, power. But there is great spiritual danger in each one of them.

The danger in this way of thinking is based in the premise that people are of value only if they fit some cultural description of what is cool. In the past twenty years, this nation has developed a national culture through marketing. Through national television and mass marketing strategies, the marketplace has become less distinct and more homogeneous. It used to be that students from New Jersey dressed differently from students in Minneapolis, that students in Southern California had their own style, which was different from that of students in Wyoming. All of that has changed. Regional styles still exist, but to a lesser degree. It is not uncommon to find the same styles on campuses all across the nation. So who gives us the culturally acceptable picture of what is cool? Who tells us what styles are in or out? And even more serious: who tells us which people are in and which are out, which people are acceptable and which are not?

Image is fine. It can even be fun. My kids have been working in recent years to update me and to turn me into the fine dresser I am today. (What they don't know is that some of the styles have finally come around full circle, so that even the beautiful ties I used to love to wear are finally back in style.) I don't have any great problem with trying on new images and even experimenting with different styles and forms, but the danger is in confusing success with the image. The danger is confusing image and substance.

What you do is important, but that is not what makes you a success, not according to biblical criteria. During my ministry I have talked to many elderly people about this issue. These people often find that they can no longer do whatever they did when they were younger, and very often they decide that they are now failures. They can no longer perform. They can no longer contribute. They are no longer productive. And a performance-based society decrees them "failures" or "worthless"!

Many college students have also concluded that they are unworthy because they don't somehow measure up to these criteria. They believe the notion that they are worthless because they don't fit the cultural standards for success. They may be driven to dishonesty to achieve success. They may be driven to binge eating and other eating disorders to fit the cultural norm. They may be driven to workaholism in order to appear to have it all.

"If you really knew me . . ." A group leader asked students to finish that sentence. Their answers varied—some deep, several funny—and then it was Julie's turn. "If you really knew me, you wouldn't like me very much." Her tears burned her face with the stinging pain of too much rejection and too many comparisons. Julie was not one of the beautiful people, and she knew it. The problem is that she also bought into the conclusions of her peers, that her worth was measured by their acceptance. By all such measures she was a failure.

How do you define success? By who you are? By what you do? Paul says, try again: you define success by *who you know.* When Paul evaluates his life he says that only one thing really counts, that he knows Jesus Christ as Lord. You may or may not be one of the beautiful people. You may or may not be a great financial success. You may or may not make it to the top of every organization with which you work, but that isn't what life is about anyway. And if that thirst for upward mobility is what drives you, then you have missed the point somewhere along the way.

Every time you begin another semester you're faced with the same question: How will you define its success? By a grade or a score? By a job or a date? By a new relationship? All are fine as means to an end. But there is more—for everyone. Make sure you don't settle for second best. Paul said, "I want to know Jesus and the power of his resurrection." When we know Jesus, at least two things become clear: we know that we are loved and valued, and we know where we are headed. We know our goal—to follow where he leads us. Eugene Peterson offers a wonderful paraphrase of Ephesians 1:14 in *The Message:* "It's in Christ that we find out who we are and what we are living for."

When Julie became a Christian, something changed for her. She actually believed what she was told about this rabbi named Jesus. She actually believed his love for her made her valuable and worthwhile. She said, "I can't say that I'm OK everyday. I still feel the pain, but I have something no one can take away from me: I know that I am loved, and that makes me somebody special."

I remember clearly sitting in a college chapel as a freshman and listening to Tom Skinner preach. He looked up at the balcony where I sat and said in his huge, deep voice, "I know who I am. I am a son of God, and no one, no one can take that away from me."

If that's true, then how do you spell success?

Questions for Groups

1. Have each member of the group identify the group they were in in high school. What were the "marks" of each group in your school?

2. What image of success did you learn from your parents?

3. Create a group definition for success based on Paul's teachings as given in this chapter.

4. Write a note to yourself to be read later in the week: "My success this week will be based on the vitality of my walk with Jesus." Pin the note on your bulletin board and open it on Wednesday.

10

When Your
Grade Is an F

Tara felt dejected and angry. For the third time in the semester she was handed an exam and the professor turned it over so the grade wouldn't show to the others. She sat in the classroom and waited until everyone was gone before she looked. There it was, again. For the third time she had failed.

If "success" means achieving all of one's goals and arriving at perfection, one is likely to fail more often than succeed. Failure is our common lot in life. We need to think about failure, to help us prepare to handle it well.

Failure is when you are deficient or perform ineffectively. It's when you perform below the grade-level minimum or when you cease functioning properly. All of these definitions, however, assume a commonly acceptable standard—and such standards simply don't exist.

Failure comes to us in many different settings. It came most strongly to me as a ninth-grader for whom the idea of algebra was an unsolved mystery. Instead of spending summer at the pool and tennis courts, I spent it trying to unlock the mysteries left locked after my first excursion through basic algebra.

Failure comes to us when we don't live up to our own moral standards or values. I suspect that we all remember times when we have let down our own standards and compromised our values. Failure comes sometimes because we are disobedient to the Word of God and its teachings. I'm not talking about the "gray" areas but those teachings that are clear and certain. Failure is missing the mark that you have set for yourself. What do you do when you don't reach your goals or when you fall short of the objectives you laid out? What do you do when your grade is an F?

Accept Your Failures

First, you need to accept your failures. In the words of the Serenity Prayer, "God, grant me the serenity to accept what cannot be changed." You must face your failure. You must dare to look it squarely in the eye and accept it. When Jesus found himself stalled in his efforts, he took the Twelve aside and sent them out two by two. After telling them to take nothing with them on their journey, he said, "If anyone will not welcome you or listen to your words, shake off the dust from your feet as you leave that house or town" (Mt 10:14). It's a strange set of directions, isn't it? "Shake off the dust from your feet." What does it mean?

Jesus meant it as a prophetic symbol. Pious Jews who traveled outside of Israel customarily removed from their sandals all the dust of the alien lands in which they had traveled. By this action they disassociated themselves from the pollution of those lands. For the disciples it was a warning that although they had fulfilled their mission, the people had rejected their message. It was also a means of accepting failure. Jesus taught the disciples to accept their failure and to move on. He wanted them to know that the time comes when you must face failure and accept it; that you must keep going on and not allow yourself to become fixed on that failure; that you cannot allow yourself the luxury of quitting when you meet disappointments.

When Peter denied Jesus for the third time, something profoundly important happened. "At that moment, while he was still speaking, the cock crowed. The Lord turned and looked at Peter. Then Peter remembered the word of the Lord, how he had said to him, 'Before the cock crows today, you will deny me three times.' And he went out and wept bitterly" (Lk 22:60-62). Mark it well—Peter *remembered*. The key to facing failure helpfully is to face it, to accept it. Peter remembered all of his certainty just a few hours before. He remembered his vow to Jesus that he could never leave him. Peter remembered his cocky confidence. He remembered all of his best intentions. And he wept bitterly. But he faced his failures. He did not deny his denial!

The only option is to deny your failures. You can block them out and repress their memory. You can live with the illusion that you are above failure. You can play the game of pass the buck: when you blow it you pass the buck to someone or something else—to a roommate, a sibling, a parent, a professor, a friend, the weather, the stars or maybe even God himself. You can pass the buck, but you'll never find the healing that Peter found as he accepted the fact of his failure, as he faced his failure.

It doesn't matter if your failure is academic, moral, spiritual or otherwise. The strategy is the same: you will benefit from your failure only if you accept it with honesty.

Step on Your Failures
The second principle is to use your failures for growth. Allow them to be stepping stones instead of stumbling blocks. Someone once wrote that "failure is not sin, faithlessness is." In other words, when you meet disappointments, you must grow from them. I happen to believe that much of the time that which can be changed in a situation is me—my attitude toward it. Humans seem to be put together so that we become what we image in our minds and attitudes. If we fail and become wrapped up in that failure, we become failures. We find ourselves trapped in the same patterns. We repeat the past, rather than change ourselves. We fail. We may even accept it, but then we don't use it as fodder for growth. And then we negate and disparage ourselves for failing again. Soon we collect failures. When any successes come along, we explain them away as rare exceptions. When any failures come along, we hold on to them. We fix our attention on those failures rather than on ourselves and how we can use them for growth.

Jeremiah was in my office just the other day. He was in a relationship that had just taken a serious nosedive. He blew it and she waved goodby. Now he sat in my office to talk it over, to get some "wisdom," he said. I told him not to be in a big hurry to find comfort and to rush into the next relationship. Stop where you are, I said, and learn what you can from this failure, and then step on it—move ahead in growth. The real failure is not in falling down, but in staying there when you have fallen.

If you don't learn from rejection, or failure, or pain, you will have wasted it. I'm no different from you; I don't like to be rejected, to fail or to hurt. These feelings drive to the very core of my self-esteem. Sometimes I react with a fury to anyone who might dare to tell me I am worthless. But sometimes I remember to step on my failure because everything in life adds to who I am, even the pain.

Jesus told the disciples to shake the dust from their failures and move on. It's good advice. Don't become caught up in your failures. Don't become condemned to repeat the past. Learn from your mistakes and move on. Didn't Paul say the same thing in Philippians? "Forgetting what lies behind, . . . I press on" (Phil 3:13-14).

When I was a ninth-grader, I had no options. My teacher identified my academic failure in four steps: It started with my first-quarter grade of C minus, followed by a second-quarter grade of D. In the third quarter I received a grade of D minus, and the crowning achievement of a final grade of F. I had no choice but to accept my failure. I couldn't hide it any longer. I had flunked algebra. But that was not the end for me. Through the good graces of a fine summer school teacher, I was able to improve that F to an A!

The Friday-Morning Ritual

Every Friday morning there is a ritual on the street where I live. Usually after some debate about whose turn it is, two containers are carefully placed out on a special altar near the street. Then some people, usually in special uniforms, come in a specially equipped vehicle to gather the contents of those two containers. Then those containers are removed from the altar at the curb and returned to their honored place in the house so that the process may be repeated a week later. Obviously, I'm talking about the garbage pickup every Friday.

I have never gone with the garbage collectors to see that my garbage gets safely delivered to the dump. I have never really said, "I want to see what happens to the remains of my life this past week. I want to guarantee that they are treated carefully." No, I am just glad that someone will take the contents far away from my home. I don't want to see the stuff again.

Failures are just like that garbage. They can be fertilizer for growth, but they sure stink if you keep them around. If you remember every failure and the feelings surrounding it, and accumulate your failures, they pile up and become a burden. A little boy was praying the Lord's Prayer with his Sunday-school class and came out with this misspoken phrase: "And forgive us our trash baskets." But he had his point. Your sins—your failures and past mistakes—are just like trash baskets that need constant emptying. We call this confession. It is one way to change that which can be changed, to empty the internal garbage from one's life.

Tara took the exam in her hands and began the process of change. She did it in a way that got her through the course. She talked with her professor and found out how to study for the next exam. She received the tutoring help she needed. She refused to let the F be the final word for her. The day before the next exam she met with a study group from class and carefully prepared. When the professor returned the exams, Tara braced herself—but this time she received the exam with the score visible right on top. What did she get? It doesn't matter, Tara knows.

Questions for Groups

1. This may be hard to do, but share with each other one of the times you have experienced failure in some area of your life.
2. What helped you best to learn from this failure?
3. Create a group definition of failure that you think Paul and Jesus would accept.
4. What happened to you last week when you opened the note you wrote about success?

11

I Am Somebody

I suspect that you have been told that you have gifts and talents. The fact that you are in college suggests that someone somewhere has already believed in you and helped you to believe in yourself. Not everyone is so fortunate. But Jesus wanted us to think about our talents and gifts and thus left a parable about those gifts. It is the parable of the talents.

In the parable, each servant is entrusted with some of the Master's resources. Eugene Peterson tells the story this way:

It's like a man going off on an extended trip. He called his servants together and delegated responsibilities. To one he gave five thousand dollars, to another two thousand, to a third one thousand, depending on their abilities. Then he left. Right off, the first servant went to work and doubled his master's investment. The second did the same. But the man with the single thousand dug a hole and carefully buried his master's money.

After a long absence, the master of those three servants came back and settled up with them. The one given five thousand dollars showed him how he had doubled his investment. His master commended him: "Good work! You did your job well. From now on be my partner."

The servant with the two thousand showed how he also had doubled his master's investment. His master commended him: "Good work! You did your job well. From now on be my partner."

The servant given one thousand said, "Master, I know you have high standards and hate careless ways, that you demand the best and make no allowances for error. I was afraid I might disappoint you, so I found a good hiding place and secured your money. Here it is, safe and sound down to the last cent."

The master was furious. "That's a terrible way to live! It's criminal to live cautiously like that! If you knew I was after the best, why did you do less than the least? The least you could have done would have been to invest the sum with the bankers, where at least I would have gotten a little interest.

"Take the thousand and give it to the one who risked the most. And get rid of this 'play-it-safe' who won't go out on a limb. Throw him out into utter darkness." (Mt 25:14-30, *The Message*)

The messages in this parable are many, but three are of greatest importance.

First, each person has a part in the kingdom of God. Paul said, "Each of us was given grace according to the measure of Christ's gift." Though the gifts are varied, each person receives them. Though people's abilities, skills and background are different, each person is needed. God has entrusted humans with what God needs to multiply his love, power, forgiveness and grace in the world. Some years ago I chaired a committee that invited a speaker to lead a conference. He signed off his acceptance letter in an arresting manner: "I'm looking forward to doing something with you in your part of the kingdom." When I read those words it made me sit up and sense the importance of my work—my part of the kingdom of God! *Our* part in the kingdom of God.

Second, each person has value in the kingdom of God. That much is clear in the parable. The failure of the servant was that he sat on his gifts. He wasn't a bad person. He wasn't a wasteful person. He was simply too careful. He didn't see that his talent was needed. "Master, I know you have high standards and hate careless ways. . . . I was afraid I might disappoint you." He was cautious, frugal and defensive. He treated his master's resources with care, to be sure, but he left them unused. The possibility of failure was more than he could bear, so he gambled on security. But he lost in the end. He was safe, but nothing changed. He was secure, but nothing grew. He was careful, but nothing happened.

He was cautious, but no lives were touched. Many perfectionists are so worried about imperfection that they never take a risk.

A professor invited to speak at a baccalaureate asked the president of the university, "Would you like me to preach on some aspect of the nature of God?" The president said, "Well, that would be all right, except that most of our students believe in God—the difficulty is they don't believe in themselves."

The research on Generation X supports this evaluation. Students are characterized by feelings of hopelessness and a deep anxiety about the future. Economic downsizing has this generation uptight and cynical about the future, in which they see their options and possibilities shrinking. Therefore, students have set for themselves the goal of survival and safety. Some see this as the generation of apathy and passivity.

To this generation, the parable speaks a sharp word of encouragement, but it comes through the back door of confrontation. The master in this parable becomes angry, upset, almost vindictive. Jesus embellishes the story enough to drive the point home: the master valued the servant more than the servant valued himself. The servant depreciated and discounted his own worth. He discounted the gift. He didn't realize how precious he was to the master. That's part of Jesus' message to the X generation: you are valued and loved. When you feel hopeless, skeptical and insignificant, Jesus' message is one of your great worth. I believe he would say to every one of us: You are too valuable to bury your gifts. I didn't create you to sit on your talents.

Brennan Manning puts this message in stark language in his book *Abba's Child: The Cry of the Heart for Intimate Belonging.*

> One of the most shocking contradictions in the American church is the intense dislike many disciples of Jesus have for themselves. They are more displeased with their own shortcomings than they would ever dream of being with someone else's. They are sick of their own mediocrity and disgusted by their own inconsistency.

Henri Nouwen believes that the greatest trap in life is self-rejection. That happens when you believe the voices that call you the "un-names": unattractive, unlovable, unworthy. You allow those voices to verify what you already feel deep within, that you are no good, after all. In *Life of the Beloved* Nouwen writes powerfully, "Self-rejection is the greatest enemy of the spiritual life because it contradicts the sacred voice that calls us the 'Beloved.' Being the Beloved constitutes the core truth of our existence."

Listen to that sacred voice that calls you "beloved." Listen to the One whose life said, "Indeed, God did not send the Son into the world to condemn the world, but in order that the world might be saved through him" (Jn 3:17). Let the voice say it to you every single day of your life: You have value in the kingdom!

The third message of the parable is that *you have a choice about the kingdom of God.* You can choose to become adventuresome, to take a risk and invest in the kingdom of God.

The servant's worst fault was that he refused to take any risks. Like the scribes and Pharisees whose lives were punctuated by calculation, prediction and caution, the servant simply didn't understand kingdom thinking. He didn't know that the universe is fruitful when one takes a risk. Nothing is ever multiplied if you are too stingy. I am convinced that the master would have rewarded him gladly even if he had used that one talent and lost it all. The judgment on him is that he didn't take the risk and enter the adventure of the kingdom. He lost what he had because he sat on it. The power he was given was removed. This is not a threat, it is simply a fact of life: use it or lose it! Jesus said it with sharpness and clarity: "For those who want to save their life will lose it, and those who lose their life for my sake, and for the sake of the gospel, will save it" (Mk 8:35).

Tony Campolo once said that "people are as young as their dreams and as old as their cynicism." I know that to be true. Some of the "oldest" people I know are twenty-year-old students who have no dreams, and some of the "youngest" people I know are excited eighty-year-olds! Dennis Benson and Stan J. Stewart's story "Moonrise" says it best.

There's a little boy in this world named Andrew. He has the body of a 15 year old, but his mind stopped growing at the age of four. His father, whose name is Barry, could not accept the fact he had a mentally retarded son. His father's disappointment and resentment grew until he had a nervous breakdown. With the help of a therapist, he began to make his way back to a love for Andrew. Andrew began to feel this and responded with delight.

At Sunday School one week, Andrew's teacher drew a connection between the rising of the sun and the moon and the constantly renewed love of God. Andrew was completely overwhelmed by the idea. He asked his father if he would sit with him and watch the moonrise.

On the night of the full moon the whole family sat on the porch facing the eastern horizon. As the moon climbed over the edge of the mountains, Andrew literally shook with excitement. Then as it moved into full view, he did something he had never done before. Andrew reached out and encircled his father in his arms. His father was completely taken by surprise and the tears began to stream down his face. Andrew continued to grip his father and said in hushed tones, "I've never seen the moonrise before, have you Dad?" His father was too moved to speak.

A few minutes passed in silence. It was as if no one in that family had seen the moonrise before. When the moon was fully launched into the sky, Andrew announced, "God keeps loving all of us you know."

What are your dreams? What do you see with your eyes of faith? God gives people talents and gifts big enough to achieve the dreams he gives when they see with faith. Your dreams are to call you to utilize gifts and talents you received long ago. One missionary said, "Before God sends you to Africa, God will put Africa in your heart." Before God sends you to the world of education or business, to medicine or to forestry, God will also begin to put dreams in you for a kingdom use of your talents and gifts. Not all work or dreams are "religious" or done in church or in church-related activities. Many of the greatest dreams are for contributions to the lives of people in very practical and helpful ways.

"God keeps loving all of us you know." One of the greatest ways God showers humans with love is by equipping them with unique and distinctive talents and gifts.

Questions for Groups

1. What have you read in the newspaper in recent days that has stirred your heart and captured your imagination?

2. Tell the group about one dream you believe that God has placed in your heart. Not everyone will necessarily have such a dream, but share together with those who do.

3. Describe one thing you love to do for people.

4. Ask how you can pray for each other this week.

12

Ordinary People

Ont of the great fears I have is of mediocrity. As a young child, I was often told that I had "great potential"—but I always sensed that expression was a tool to motivate me to something more and not necessarily an accurate assessment of my abilities. I often wondered what would happen if I never lived up to that potential. What if I became simply average? What if all those who believed in me became disappointed that I never quite produced what they thought they saw in me? In fact, a friend who knew me well sent me a card one time that said, "There's nothing worse in life than to be saddled with a great potential."

Mediocrity usually comes from giving in. You settle back and give in to the lowest common denominator. You simply quit trying to fly and settle for walking or crawling. But the reality is that few people are the singular leaders of the world. What if you never become the Einstein or Schweitzer or Harriet Tubman of history? Being ordinary should not be confused with mediocrity.

Katy was upset. She sat in tears as she described her problem. "My roommate was just elected president of the sophomore class, my brother just made the dean's list, and there's a story about my sister in the paper back home because of her last track meet. And then there's me. The problem with me is that I don't do anything that is spectacular. I'm just too ordinary."

Most people are ordinary, or average, which is what it means. For these people the biblical character of Andrew should be a great example and role model. Peter Marshall called him the "Saint of the Rank and File." Not many people will become world-renowned leaders, but those are not the only people that God uses. Leadership and leadership development are important, but everyone is a follower and involved behind the scenes in one organization or another. Marshall thinks of everyone as an Andrew sitting in a class or at church. In *Mr. Jones, Meet the Master* he writes:

> You see, it is the [one-talent] Andrews after all who carry on the work of the nation and of the church. For after all the five-talent men and women have flashed like meteors through the skies leaving behind a trail of glory, after their great gifts for organization, after all their visions and their plans they depend upon Andrew to do the job.

It was to the Andrews of the world that Jesus uttered those words that came to be called "the Great Commission": "Go therefore and make disciples of all nations, baptizing them in the name of the Father and of the Son and of the Holy Spirit, and teaching them to obey everything that I have commanded you" (Mt 28:19-20).

My friends Larry and Cindy Marshall are the only white family in an African-American inner city neighborhood on Chicago's South Side. They were a farm couple living in northern South Dakota until they answered the call to go to Africa and serve God. They used their knowledge of agriculture and evangelism to help the people there. After their return to the United States they resumed farming. One day Larry went into the house and said, "Cindy, I have something to tell you." She looked him in the eye and said, "Larry, I know." He was confused. "You can't know what I'm about to tell you." She said, "Larry, I know." "But how could you know? I haven't told you yet." And Cindy said, "I know, God wants us to move to the inner city." Soon after that they moved to Chicago.

The Marshalls are not unusually gifted as speakers. They are not unusually gifted as organizers or as visionaries. They are not unusually talented as fundraisers. They are not unusually gifted except in one way: they have the great gift of faith and obedience. They bought the vacant lot next to their home and built a playground, complete with a basketball court. Now the neighborhood kids gather there to play and hear about Jesus. Larry and Cindy regularly deal with the violence and challenges of a drug-infested community, but just try to jar them loose from that foothold in the city! They will go only when God calls them to leave. Cindy put it this way, "I don't know if we are so unusual; I just happen to think others might have turned God down until he finally got to us way down on the list." But because they are there an entire neighborhood has been introduced to the name of Jesus Christ. They are a remarkable couple—mostly because they are so ordinary! The Andrew Principle at work.

You Can't Force the Heart

What is needed to be an Andrew? In *Weavings* Sue Monk Kidd tells a story of her twelfth summer:

> I had gone to a nursing home with a youth group from my church. Frankly, I was there under duress. My mother had not heard my pleas that I be spared the unjust sentence of visiting a nursing home when my friends were enjoying the last day of summer vacation at the city swimming pool. Smarting from the inequity, I stood before this ancient-looking woman, holding a bouquet of crepe paper flowers. Everything about her saddened me—the worn-down face, the lopsided grin, the tendrils of gray hair protruding from a crocheted lavender cap. I thrust the bouquet at her. She looked at me, a look that pierced me to the marrow of my 12-year-old bones. Then she spoke the words I haven't forgotten for nearly 30 years. "You didn't want to come, did you, child?"

> The words stunned me. They were too painful, too powerful, too naked in their honesty. "Oh, yes, I wanted to come," I protested.

> A smile lifted one side of her mouth. "It's okay," she said. "You can't force the heart."

> I tried to forget her. For a while I hated her for the rebuke. Then I passed it off as the harmless twittering of an old woman. Years later

though, as I began to follow the labyrinth of my spiritual journey, I discovered the truth in her words.

You can't force the heart. Genuine compassion cannot be imposed from without. It doesn't happen simply by hearing a sermon on love, or being sent on a loving mission. . . . You don't arbitrarily make up your mind to be compassionate so much as you choose to follow a journey that transforms your heart into a compassionate space.

After several days in a course on urban studies Sarah came to me and said, "I'm feeling very discouraged."

"Why?" I asked.

"Because people here have been so nice to me. Everywhere we've gone, people have been helpful and kind."

"Why is that discouraging?" I asked.

"Well, because of these people," she said. By "these people" she meant people of color, particularly African-Americans she had met on the train. "Well, because, my family and my church have taught me to be suspicious of them, not to trust them. I'm not discouraged about them, I'm discouraged because I didn't know I was that way too."

What happened to Sarah is my vision for every Christian college student. She discovered truth about herself, and compassion was born in her. Through a compassionate heart the ordinary person touches the world and its pain. Because of the compassion of that carpenter from Nazareth people find the courage to stand up as an Andrew in the harsh world of today. You see, the Andrews of this world are the many "invisible" people who are there every day, doing their job with joy. Most of them will not stand in the spotlight or see their names on the front page of the morning paper for an award, but they are some of Jesus' choice and greatest disciples.

One of those people for me was a man named Chuck. He was a custodian at the company where I worked during college. I would meet him nearly every day back at the dumpster where our routes for emptying trash would take us. He was a gentle and quiet man with a compassion for people that shone through his inquisitive eyes. Always he wanted to know what I had learned in school the previous day.

Always he asked me how I was doing, and he said it in a way that told me he really wanted to know. In time I learned that Chuck, an uneducated African-American janitor, was an Andrew to me and to many others in our building. He had a gift from God to see the world with wise eyes. I found myself looking to him for guidance when I had tough questions to answer or complicated decisions to make. Always he would answer me with a question that got me looking toward an answer. This Andrew taught me to see the world with far more inclusive and compassionate eyes than I ever had before. The "altar" of learning and finding wisdom was a shipping dock and a dumpster.

Questions for Groups

1. Identify an Andrew from your past. What role did he or she play in your life?

2. Do you know an Andrew now? Try hard to identify an Andrew in your college or university, maybe even in your own small group. Thank this person for their contribution to the lives of people around them.

3. Who has taught you the most about compassion and love for other people?
What characteristics or qualities do you admire most in that person?

4. Pray for growth in compassion for each member of your group.

13

What You Get
Is What You See

Rachel was a young mother, a student in a class I taught on Christian theology. As the course progressed and we had the opportunity to talk, I began to learn about her life. What I learned wasn't good. Her life had been marked by abuse at the hands of men. She had been sexually abused as a child by her father, physically abused as a young bride by a man who would tie her up and whip her with a cord, and harassed by a male professor. She came into the course cautious about me because of my role as a campus pastor, and very, very angry at God.

What Rachel believed about God she had learned from the men in her life. Over the semester she began to learn some basic theological truths about the nature, character and identity of God. These new images of God challenged her former images. The final paper for the course was to be a ten-page statement of the student's theological beliefs. Read carefully what Rachel said. (She gave me permission to use this.)

Dear Keith, all semester you've been asking for personal opinions, reflections, and feelings about the material we've covered in class. As you probably know by now, I have an extremely hard time expressing myself. The problem is that, for the past nine years or more, I've been told that everything I've said or even thought was incredibly stupid and wrong—so don't say anything. I was led to believe that my thoughts and opinions did not matter and I became very withdrawn. My self-esteem was beaten to a pulp and I was humiliated at every opportunity for just being me. I soon started hating myself. I thought God hated me too, if there was a God, and that I was being punished by an angry, cruel God who regarded me as worthless.

Because of this class and everything you have taught me, I can now see that I had things turned around. God did not hate me; I hated me. God did not consider me worthless; I did. God was not angry; I was. The punishment came from an abusive man, not from God. My impression of God was that of a heavenly tyrant. He was a cruel, unpredictable, vindictive God.

She then describes in great detail the changes that came about in her life as she modified her thinking about the character and nature of God. For the first time in her life she discovered God as One who was on her side, who loved her and who believed in her. That brought a transformation of her own self-worth, self-esteem and self-respect.

What Rachel saw and believed about the character of God shaped much of her life. The images of God that she carried came from an abusive father, a cruel husband, an indifferent church. A very basic principle of the universe is at work in all of this: people become, in a very real sense, what they see. The old adage "What you see is what you get" is not all that inaccurate.

The apostle John gives a startling portrait of God in the first chapter of his Gospel. He says that God is so in love with us that he wants to move into our neighborhood. In the man Jesus we see the human face of God, whose love compels him to move in down the street!

His tent is glorious. And more—it is full of the two things that you need: grace and truth. Grace to know you are loved and to know someone believes in you. The truth about yourself, about life and about God. "From his fullness we have all received, grace upon grace. The law indeed was given through Moses; grace and truth came through Jesus Christ" (Jn 1:16-17).

If you look at God but don't see the love and relentless tenderness of Jesus, then you must look again. If you see judgment and law and rules and restrictions and penalties and discipline, then look again. Do

> **Truths About Jesus from John 1**
> He always was with God (v. 2).
> He created everything that is (v. 3).
> He is life and life is found in him (v. 4).
> His life lights up the neighborhood for everyone, and the darkness of the neighbors will never put it out (v. 4).
> He came to his own people, the Jews. He came back to his old neighborhood, and they didn't accept him (v. 11).
> He comes to anyone who needs a family. His is the acceptance of a home and real love (v. 12).
> The rising crescendo of the chapter is that he literally pitched his tent down the street. He moved into the neighborhood (v. 14).

what my friend Rachel did: take a second look.

Brennan Manning has one of the most riveting personalities of anyone I have ever met. His life is an open testimony to one who has faced both failure and success, suffering and glory, defeat and hope. Most of all it is an open testimony to one who has discovered the incarnate Jesus walking into every part of his world. In his book *The Ragamuffin Gospel* he powerfully illustrates the truth that God loves us with an unrelenting love. His stories and his teachings are arresting as they tell us one basic truth: God is desperately in love with us!

This truth comes in a prophetic word spoken by Jesus to a thirty-four-year-old widow, Marjory Kempe, in Lynn, Massachusetts. The message that she received in 1667 remains ever ancient, ever new: "More pleasing to me than all your prayers, works, and penances is that you would believe I love you."

Manning retells a story from a Bahamian priest that captures the essence of biblical trust:

A two-story house had caught on fire. The family—father, mother, several children—were on their way out when the smallest boy became terrified, tore away from his mother, ran back upstairs. Suddenly he appeared at a smoke-filled window crying like crazy.

His father, outside, shouted: "Jump, son, jump! I'll catch you." The
boy cried: "But, daddy, I can't see you." "I know," his father called,
"I know. But I can see you."
That's the leap of faith—to the arms of a loving parent whom you
cannot see, but who sees you and calls you to jump in trust.

It's as practical as this question: do you rely on your résumé or on
the gospel of grace?

Grace tells us that we are accepted just as we are. We may not be the
kind of people we want to be, we may be a long way from our goals,
we may have more failures than achievements, we may not be
wealthy or powerful or spiritual, we may not even be happy, but we
are nonetheless accepted by God, held in his hands. Such is his
promise to us in Jesus Christ, a promise we can trust. (*The Ragamuffin
Gospel*)

Recently a student friend said to me, "For the twenty years of my life I
have never heard the gospel as God intended it." Curious, I pressed
him for more. He answered, "Only now do I hear it as God intends
it—it is good news. News of freedom and joy and trust and love and
forgiveness and acceptance and grace." God has put out a welcome mat
for us, but too often we're like the little boy who, when asked if he could
read it, said, "Sure. It says, wipe your feet." No! It doesn't say wipe your
feet. It says welcome—that's the grace. And it opens the door to
holiness—that's the truth.

Because in his love God is lurking about to give you grace at every
turn, you are now called to participate in an ongoing incarnation of
making the Word flesh in others' lives. Because Jesus moved into your
neighborhood, he invites you to move into the world as neighbor to
others.

Answer this question for yourself: What is your dominant impression
or image of God? What's the word picture or conceptual picture you
carry around of the character and nature of God? Tell yourself the
truth. Is "your" God angry or uptight or scary or ready to bring
suffering or to impose laws? Or have you discovered the God whose
love is unending and unconditional?

When he visited on our campus Brennan Manning asked us to

imagine that we were invited to sit in the lap of Abba-God. *Abba* was Jesus' name for God. It is a term of endearment, affection and love. He asked us to consider over and over again what it feels like to have God's arms hold us in tenderness and grace. All during the next year my friend Tim would shout at me as he passed me in the hall: "Remember where you are, Keith, remember where you are." Immediately I would see myself seated on the lap of Abba-God, on the lap of One who loves me with an intense and abiding love.

Rachel's life was actually transformed because she looked again at her portrait of God. The picture that was hanging in the hallway of her life was defective. It stifled her life and kept her locked up in self-contempt and pain. But when she looked again and saw a new portrait of this surprising, startling, unexpected God with a human face whose name is Jesus, her world was transformed. She began to love herself and then, cautiously, the world around her. What does the portrait in the hallway of your life look like?

Questions for Groups
1. Create a group definition of grace.
2. Describe your most recent experience of grace. Who was involved? What did they do? How did it make you feel?
3. What is your dominant image of God? (Is God an angry or judgmental God? Is God a loving and tender God? Is God a pushover who lets people get away with things? Or is God the God who pursues people relentlessly in love, as Brennan Manning believes?)
4. Pray for the person seated on your right. Pray that God will bring him or her the gift of grace in a very practical way in the week ahead.

14

You Can't Be Choosy About Parents

I finished my college classes in May and was planning to be married in August. Like any intelligent, discerning and fiscally responsible person with a calculator, I figured out that I could save a lot of money if I lived at home that summer. That way I could let my parents pay for a few things—like rent, food, insurance, car payments, gas and oil, tuxedo. So home I went.

I saw myself as an adult—and more mature than anyone else my age! But when I got home I found my parents being typical parents—wanting to know when I'd be home and where I was going. When I came home late after a night out with the guys, my mother was asleep on the sofa with the brown plaid blanket wrapped around her—waiting up for me just like when I was in high school. Mom was treating me in the same old ways, and I was ready for a change in our relationship. But how could I make that happen?

The title of this chapter points out what we already know: of all the things you have some control over in life, choosing your parents isn't one of them. But while you don't get to pick your parents, you do have some choice in how to deal with them.

Honor My Parents?
Exodus 20:12 says, "Honor your father and your mother." Traditionally, Christians have used these words to coerce kids to obey their parents.

But they were first spoken to the whole covenant community, not exclusively to children. At the foot of Mount Sinai were three distinct groups of people who made the long trek from Egypt: the active working men and women, the little ones and the elderly, who were no longer able to carry their own loads. To which of these groups did God give his laws? To all of them—the great majority of whom were adults. Moses is saying to them, honor your adult parents. That means these words are meant for you.

What does it mean to honor your parents? Two words are important: respect and value. The basic value inherent in this commandment is that parents are due the respect of their children. The statement "It is because a human being is precious in the sight of God that a person is to be respected" is true, but it is not enough. God calls people to respect their parents, to honor them in the Lord as Paul says in Ephesians 6:1. Why? Because one's respect for parents is a sign of respect for God. Christians honor their parents because they honor God and God's Word instructs them to do so. Bowing to the higher authority of God, Christians thus honor their parents as a sign of submission to the Creator. What difference would it make if you began to treat your parents as God's beloved children, even if they are not the world's most perfect parents? What might happen if you began to see them as people about whom God cares?

To honor doesn't mean to obey blindly, but to respect. Martin Luther King Jr. preached nonviolent civil disobedience. He taught people to disobey the immoral laws of the government, but he always preached respect for authority. Even when imprisoned unjustly, beaten cruelly and oppressed unmercifully, he continued to teach respect. Sometimes you may honor the position more than you are able to honor the person in that position. Thus, some people honor the place of parents in God's scheme more than they can honor a particular parent.

Genesis 2:24 says, "Therefore a man leaves his father and his mother and clings to his wife." The time will come when a man or a woman needs to leave home. But God does not intend for them to turn their backs on this duty to honor their parents. Some people honor their parents and never leave them; they never cut the cord and get on with their own lives. Others leave their parents and no longer honor them.

Second, to honor is to value. You should value your parents not only because of what they can give you but for the gift they are to life itself. The fifth commandment thunders forth that your value is not found in who you are or in what you can do; your value is a God-given gift. In a book titled *Aging,* Henri Nouwen speaks of elderly parents and says, "There can hardly be a more alienating feeling than that which believes, 'I am who I was.'" Your value is in who you are—a child of God. In the ancient nomadic societies life was spent wandering from sparse grazing land to water holes. The climate was harsh: hot, scorching heat in the daytime and piercing cold at night. The temptation (and in some places the practice) was to leave behind those who could no longer keep up with the caravan. Many unwanted, no longer productive parents were left to die in the desert. But God's Word says no! Honor your adult parents, respect them and value them.

You Don't Know My Parents

In an introductory speech course a few years ago a female student spoke about repeated sexual abuse from her father during her teen years. Immediately after the speech several other young women approached her and said, "I know what you're talking about. I've been through it too."

In my time in Christian higher education, I have probably talked to students about this issue more than any other. The fact of widespread abuse has to influence the application of teachings such as honoring one's parents. Some parents simply are not honorable people. They have abused their children just as they have abused their responsibilities before God as parents. Some of you have not been abused directly, but instead know the dull ache of neglect. Your parents have been too busy, too indifferent, too uncaring. So how do you apply these teachings in all of these varied situations? How can you really apply this to your relationship with your parents?

I offer two thoughts. They may sound contradictory at first, but give them a chance to sink in. For some of you, this will only be a little of the information you need; if so, I hope you will find someone to talk to.

First, expect *less* of your parents. Realize that your parents are human, and no humans are perfect. All parents fail their children. They make mistakes, sometimes mistakes that will scar you for life. But remember, they too may have been scarred by others. Expect less of your parents in the sense that your parents may have given you all they know how to give. They may not know how to be the parents you had hoped they would be. And remember that parents are people in need of forgiveness and grace too.

Second, expect *more* of your parents. Begin to relate to them as adult to adult. The emotional business we have with our parents varies from person to person. Some of you need to express gratitude to your parents for what they have done for you and what they have given to you. When was the last time you said thank you to your parents for all the times that they've been there for you and with you?

Remember that your parents are people too! They have dreams, ideas, goals, fears and worries, just like you do. When my son was in college and home for the summer he took me out to a coffee shop. We sat with our cappucino and enjoyed a beautiful summer evening. After a while he asked, "So tell me, what keeps you interested in your work?" This was not our normal type of conversation! I looked at him in curiosity and realized that he was serious. I wasn't used to being asked that kind of question by my own children, but it was a beginning. It was his initiative that started a process of relating as adult to adult.

Some of you may need to forgive your parents for what they did or failed to do in your life. Everyone must come to terms with his or her own imperfections and the imperfections of others. Doing so, you may need to forgive your parents for how they have failed you.

A Letter Home

At the age of twenty-two, in my first year of seminary, I heard Howard Clinebell speak about unfinished business—of people whose parents died before they could complete their "business" with them. He spoke of words that needed to be said, touches that needed to be given, gestures and symbols that needed to be shared.

I left that lecture hall, went to the library and began to write. Two hours and eight pages later, I was done. I said all that I had needed to say for years to my parents. I told them of ways I felt scarred and cheated, hurt by the process of life, grieved by decisions made and directions taken. I dropped the letter into the mailbox and then fell into a cold sweat. I lived in terror for three days. *What if they reject me totally? What if they become enraged at my blatant honesty? What if they call? What if they don't call?*

But they did—and in the longest phone conversation we'd ever had, they responded. Without defensiveness they told of their hurts and pain and sadness too. They spoke of their mistakes and mine, and we forgave one another. I turned a corner that day and have never seen my parents in the same way again.

Not everyone can write *and* send such a letter. Not all parents can handle such a confrontation with the maturity, wisdom and gentleness that mine did. For some, just writing the letter may be the step needed. You may need to reveal such feelings slowly and carefully over time.

I used to meet with a certain student before every major holiday. Going home for her was traumatic, painful and sometimes disastrous. She did not look forward to semester break or holidays, as her parental home was a place of pain and anger. So we would meet for a strategy session before she left for home. I suggested that she identify one thing she needed to say to her parents during the time she was home. Eventually she began to see some change in her parents' treatment of her.

Some parents, however, are alcoholic or emotionally abusive. Some have sexually and physically abused their children, and the stakes are too high for such a confrontation. If those descriptions fit your family, perhaps what you need to do is distance yourself and claim the unique independence you need to be yourself. Some parents have an instinct to dominate and control. If you allow that domination you will never be a fully functioning adult. Some people need to leave their father and mother and grow up, to assume responsibility for their own choices and existence. And some of us, maybe all of us, need resolve to find ways to be a healthy part of a future relationship with parents.

When my grandmother died my dad walked up the stairs and told me. We stood on the stairway, and he hugged me as I cried and cried. Someday that man will die too, and I will hold my children and cry with them. And then will come the day when it is my turn and I will stand with my other Father, God my parent. When I do, I will want him to know that I honored him in the way I honored my father and my mother.

Questions for Groups

1. What is your relationship with your parents like today? How do you feel about them, and how do they feel about you?

2. What is the greatest contribution your parents have made to your life?

3. What is the greatest difficulty you currently have with your parents?

4. Ask how you can pray for each other's relationship with parents in the week ahead.

15

Judy's Little Brother

Some time ago, I began a chapel service by asking those who were the oldest in their family to stand. They stood with confidence and certainty—they were, after all, the oldest, the responsible ones. Then I asked those born in the middle to stand. There was some noise. Many looked around to see if others had stood yet, but finally this group stood. And then I asked for all those born last to stand, and pandemonium broke out! There were cheers and hoots and hollering. It was a party! They were, after all, the youngest. All three groups fit the description of their place in the birth order. And it was fascinating to see their emotions as I talked about families.

Being a part of my family meant following in the footsteps of Judy Anderson. When I started high school every teacher seemed to know about this wonderful wizard of academics whose name appeared, it seemed, on every honor roll, dean's list and advanced-placement class register. The only teacher who didn't know her was the one in charge of afternoon detention hall. I had the distinction of knowing her well.

Your family complaints and issues may be different from mine. Family life doesn't fit a single description any longer, if it ever did. Increasingly, more people grow up in blended families with parents from divorces and siblings from other marriages. Others grow up in single-parent families, most often headed by a woman. Even the traditional two-parent families have changed enormously due to the high increase in two-job families. Everyone responds to discussion about family in different ways—some project pain, others joy. But the reality is our families are a part of us.

Family Ties

In the weeks or months that you're away from your family you can begin to grow and enter into a more adult relationship with them, or you can return home just as you left. What will surprise you, however, is that the people you left behind will have done some growing on their own too. The college years offer one of the greatest opportunities for growth with your family. On campus you may have the opportunity to meet new "brothers and sisters" in Jesus Christ and to develop healthy relationships with them. What you learn from good friends can become part of your relationships at home. You can bring home new perspectives, new joys, new ideas, even new depth of faith. But take your time and be patient with your family when you first get home.

Christopher's Christmas break didn't go very well. His family expected him to come back just as he had left, but he wasn't ready to return to a dependent, parent-child relationship. After all, for nearly four months he'd been in charge of his life, and yet his family seemed to think that everything should be just like it was in August. For the first few days everyone treated him like a visitor, a guest. It was wonderful. He felt important and found that everyone wanted to know all about his life. But then things settled back into "normal." At first he was upset because they didn't seem as interested in him, but then it dawned on him: he had been home four days and hadn't yet asked about *them*. He had been so busy telling them all about *his* life that he had forgotten that they had lives too. As he showed increased interest in his mother and sisters, he found their interest in him returned. He remembered that his family's life had gone on and grown too while he was away.

The saddest situation of all is the family that doesn't grow, that simply stays "as we always were." You never change. You never grow. You simply move on, wear new clothes and finally move away in bitterness and frustration.

Lessons in Family Life

Remember, first, that these people will be your family for a long time! Even in divorce, your father and mother remain your parents, your siblings remain your family. You may choose never to speak to one or all of them again, but this relationship is lifelong. You may need to make it a priority to build a positive, healthy relationship with them.

Second, building a healthy relationship with your family requires communication. You need to call or write to them on a regular basis, so that they won't feel rejected. Remember to communicate with your siblings and to include them in your phone calls or visits too.

Third, treat your family as those whom God cares about. Didn't Jesus say, "Do unto others as you would have them do unto you"? Do you think he meant that principle for everyone except your family? Treat them as you want them to treat you, even if they're not great as a family, even if they're not themselves Christians and even if they can't quite get it all figured out.

Fourth, help them to feel a part of your college life. It's not their fault that they don't know the lingo. If they show any interest in it, teach them the campus jargon. They may never be as cool as you are, but give them a chance to try.

Finally, where there is conflict, handle it with respect. Families are notoriously cruel to each other because everyone knows that the family is forever. However, the American culture is increasingly violent, as conflicts are handled with guns or knives rather than with patience and respectful words. As a Christian you are under new management, and the management team expects you to "speak the truth in love."

Forgive and Forget

It's not always easy to resolve conflicts. Some of you need to forgive a family member for something. Some of you need to ask forgiveness from a family member. Some of you need to communicate in new patterns and new ways with your family. Thanksgiving, Christmas, quarter and semester breaks all provide great laboratories for experiments like these. Get on with it!

It has been said that bitterness is not something that is done to you, it is something you do to yourself because of what has been done to you. Bitterness is a response to the pain that others have unjustly caused you. Paul has a strong response: "Forgetting what lies behind and straining forward to what lies ahead, I press on toward the goal for the prize of the heavenly call of God in Christ Jesus" (Phil 3:13-14).

Should you ignore the past? No, that is a lie. Should you pretend it never happened? No, that is a lie too. However, you need to "forget" the past by letting it go. With helpful counsel or strong support from others or through prayer you can "forget" the hurt and put your energy into a new beginning with those who hurt you. Don't let the past tie you up or tie you down. Move toward a new future, and find growth instead of bitterness!

Finally, hang in there with your family. Don't ever give up on them. Families are people-in-process and are capable of growth and development. Share some of what you've been learning on campus and invite them into the new world of your ideas, values and thoughts.

Questions for Groups

1. Share with each other some biographical information. (How many brothers or sisters do you have? What kind of childhood relationship did you have with each of them?)

2. What is your relationship with your family now? How do you feel about it?

3. What is one practical thing you can do in the next twenty-four hours that will be a gift of love for your family?

4. Pray for your families as a group.

16

He's Different

He's different," she said. I knew what she meant. I had seen the looks before, I had felt the slam of judgment before. I knew exactly what she meant. Different is not cool. Different is bad.

I lived all of my childhood years knowing the pain of prejudice. During the birth process for my older brother Jerry, my mother went into a convulsion that crimped the umbilical cord and cut off the flow of oxygen to his brain. The result is that he was brain damaged at birth. Nobody knew that for sure until he was about four, when he began to show signs that he wasn't normal. In fact, he was different. As his life passed, it became apparent to everyone that he was "mentally retarded." That was the most clinical term I knew as a child. I also knew every other hateful word the other kids used to describe him: "SPED," "retard," "dummy," "stupid." Everywhere we went I experienced for him, and sometimes with him, the pain of prejudice. It came across racial, economic, cultural and gender lines. He was mocked and abused in public by people who were uncomfortable with his differentness.

Because he has the mental skills of about a six-year-old child, Jerry's life is limited, which has affected my family in profound ways that we still continue to unpack today. At times, especially when I was a high-school student, my embarrassment led me to be ashamed of him. I was ashamed of my own brother because he was different. Because of something that happened to him at birth that was beyond his control.

All of my life I lived with the walls created by people in response to one fact: Jerry is different. I can deal quite well with the curious and innocent stares and questions of children who wonder why he looks like he does or does what he does, or why he doesn't always answer someone with an intelligent response. But the adults who ridicule or run, who mock or say hurtful things, are harder for me to accept.

Reconciliation and Grace

The world has learned to function quite efficiently behind all kinds of walls. You see it on campus every day. The first thing Bill noticed when he walked into the cafeteria was that all of the black students sat at one table, while the Asian students met in another corner. Scattered throughout were groups of white students clustered together. He asked this question: "Does our faith say anything at all about the subtle racism we see around us? What does the Bible say to us about prejudice, racial attitudes, and racially biased practices?"

In the dorm that night, a Bible study group studied a text in Ephesians. Two of the leaders set up the event. They asked Angela, the only black student in the group, to go along with them in an exercise. When the study started they said, "Tonight's passage is about racial relationships, and it seems like it will be pretty awkward with Angela as the only black student here tonight, so we need to ask her to leave." The group sat in stunned silence as Angela left and the leaders started the study.

The leaders then talked about how Jesus broke down the dividing wall of hostility and brought reconciliation. The group members were concerned about Angela, but no one said a word. They just waited for someone else to do something, but no one did. The leaders said, "What does this text say about our racial attitudes?" There was complete silence. Finally, the leaders told the group that they had set up this experience and that Angela was in on the plot. She came back into the room, and they got into Paul's teachings with renewed energy and

---

Removing Barriers

I doubt I will ever forget the story I heard of another kind of barrier, the barrier of one who lived his life in a wheelchair after a tragic accident. He was invited, along with his wife, to a costume party at his church, but it happened to fall near the anniversary of his accident and he was feeling pretty low at that time. When the invitation came he felt even worse. "How can I go to a costume party? I'm sure no one will know who is the one guy sitting in the wheelchair. It's a joke. I won't go." But his wife coaxed him until the night arrived. He was angry that night and almost backed out but went anyway. When he got to the church, what he saw was like nothing he had ever thought possible. Every man in that group had rented a wheelchair and was there in costume. You see what they did? They acted to remove the barrier in order to love him.

---

group opened the door for learning.

In Ephesians 2 Paul writes about a gift that Jesus has given, a tool that will break down walls and open doors between people: his grace. Jesus' acceptance comes to people in their sin, not in spite of their sin. "While we were yet sinners, Christ showed us grace because he died for us." Not just for a few but for all. And then Paul says not to take that for granted, but to remember who you were—aliens, outsiders, separated from Christ because of your sin. You were once those who didn't have the faintest idea of Christ. The tool that Jesus gives is the key of grace—grace that he gives and grace that he expects you to give too.

Christ brought us together through his death on the Cross. The Cross got us to embrace, and that was the end of the hostility. Christ came and preached peace to you outsiders and peace to us insiders. He treated us as equals and so made us equals. Through him we both share the same Spirit and have equal access to the Father.

That's plain enough, isn't it? You're no longer wandering exiles. The Kingdom of faith is now your home country. You're no longer strangers or outsiders. You *belong* here, with as much right to the name Christian as anyone. God is building a home. He's using us all—irrespective of how we got there—in what he is building. (Eph 2:13-18 in Eugene Peterson, *The Message*)

Society has since learned from the Berlin Wall that it is easier to break down brick and mortar walls than it is to break down the Berlin Walls in the hearts and minds of people. Most of these walls are built in our heads as we grow up.

Jesus Didn't Look like That!

I remember visiting Keystone Baptist Church in Chicago when I was a child. There was a picture of Jesus on the wall: it was just like one we had at home, except that this Jesus was black! It was wrong—Jesus didn't look like that—Jesus wasn't like that—Jesus had long, light-brown hair, blue eyes and white skin. I knew that! I knew that because my church told me so. I knew that because every picture I ever saw showed that kind of Jesus. No one told me that in so many words, but they taught me that anyway. And now I faced a wall—these people, these different people thought Jesus looked like them!

When I asked my questions, the tragedy is that no one told me the truth—that Jesus looked more like the Jesus of color than the Swede in my front hallway.

Children don't start out rejecting others—they learn that from adults. Children aren't born racist—they become racist. Children aren't born sexist—adults make them sexist. Children don't start out afraid of differences—they are curious and ready to celebrate them.

Paul says to us that Christ brought us together through his death on the cross. He treated us as equals and so made us equals. He gave us all access to the Father and to the Spirit. Do you think that God is pleased that Sunday morning at eleven o'clock is still the most segregated hour in the week? Do you think that God is pleased that churches still operate as all white, all black, all Asian, all Hispanic, all Native American?

Jesus tears down the walls, and we spend our lives building them back up all over again.

Ramon told me what it's like to be a Hispanic male in a predominantly white college. "I felt out of place when I arrived. The culture was different. The way people communicated was different. The food was different, and even the clothes were different." I asked him how he got through, and was saddened by his answer: "I changed my behavior to fit in. I became like the people around. I quit being Hispanic."

There was not an intentional conspiracy to mold him into a new person, but the differences felt so great that, in time, Ramon did what he needed to do to fit in. Only now, after graduation, is he trying to recover his own ethnic and cultural identity.

The story of my brother and his traumatic birth was almost repeated when my youngest son was born. After long hours of labor, a crisis arose in the birth process. Kristoffer was trying to enter the world seat first with the umbilical cord wrapped around his neck. A young black intern coming in for a routine check quickly shouted orders. He physically stopped the birth of my son and saved him from the same fate as his uncle. Our Hispanic physician, Dr. Garcia, performed an emergency Caesarean section, assisted by two Filipino nurses, a Chinese anesthesiologist and one white nurse.

Do you think that I stopped to discuss their racial history with any of them? Do you think that I worried about their qualifications because they weren't white like I was? Of course not. I thanked them then, and I thank God for them every year on my son's birthday when I remember that God brought together this rainbow team to bring him safely into the world.

Racism, sexism, ageism, genderism, religious or political elitism, economic elitism—all of these want to build back the walls that Jesus has knocked down. They want us to treat each other based on our culture, gender, race and economic status. But Jesus said, "You are no longer strangers and aliens, but citizens together."

Howard Thurman, a black preacher, writer and university chaplain and one of my most important mentors, said that the greatest cause of racism in our nation is that we have contact without fellowship. We see each other, but don't live together. We ride the same bus, but don't talk. We shop in the same stores, but don't relate. We go to the same schools, but we remain segregated from one another. Yet Jesus calls us to new relationships. I call this the principle of intentionality. You intend to learn what you can about each other. You start with an interest in the differences rather than a judgment of them. You have to work at it.

Such walls need to be torn down on our campuses today. Does it matter where and with whom you sit in the dining center? Does it matter whom you include and whom you exclude? Does it matter whether or not you tell ethnic jokes and stories? Does it matter if you assume that you know how others feel and what their experience is? Does it matter if you build friendships across racial and cultural lines? Just ask Angela and the other students in that Bible study. They'll tell you!

Questions for Groups

1. What kinds of "different" people make you the most uneasy or uncomfortable? Why?

2. Describe one experience with a person from a different group, race or culture. How did you feel about that person and the experience?

3. Find an article in the newspaper about racism and discuss a Christian response to each of the people involved in the situation.

4. Pray for the unity of the group and for a growing sensitivity to others in the community.

17

The Coming Race Wars?

Several guys were standing around after chapel. The speaker, a black leader who talked about racism as he had experienced it in his college years, had upset them, and they wanted to talk. The first student said, "Isn't this 'racial stuff' all just part of the movement of political correctness?" Another said, "After all, Jesus didn't have anything to say about race or racism, did he?" The third said, more angrily, "Look, I'm tired of hearing about race and racism. It has nothing to do with me! I don't have any problems with people of other races. I even have people of other races on my floor, and they don't bother me at all." The last guy said, "I just want to deal with the spiritual issues and talk about things that concerned Jesus. He wasn't as concerned about all this race stuff. He didn't make such a big deal about it, did he?"

Well, I think he did. Even in his day there were ethnic, social, political and theological barriers. One day Jesus was in Judea, which is in the south, and he needed to get back north to Galilee. John writes that Jesus went through Samaria. The Samaritans were a group of people whom the Jews considered less than pure Jews. They considered them to be unclean—ritually speaking. To the Jews, the Samaritans were the outsiders. Symbolically, they are those you find it hardest to love because somebody told you they were bad or scary or dangerous. They are people you think instinctively that you cannot trust or befriend. They are enemies whom you disrespect and avoid.

So when Jesus went to Samaria, he taught his followers what it means to be kingdom people. He did not *have* to go through Samaria, but he chose to go that way. He did not *have* to go through this difficult part of the land or to face the traditional enemies of his people, but he chose to do so. In his actions, Jesus challenged the very real ethnic, nationalistic and gender barriers that stood between people in his day. His three-part agenda included those habits of the heart that kept people from one another.

First, Jesus illustrated an image of God that everyone needs. Jesus came to reconcile people to God and to one another. What shocked the disciples is that Jesus really meant it. His encounter with the Samaritan woman at the well is a prime example (Jn 4). From the start, Jesus gave dignity to the woman by asking for her help. He wanted to reach out to her with living water, but he was not above asking her to help him. He treated her as someone who had something that he needed.

Very often in the drive to be helpful, we destroy the dignity of others. We do that when we are willing to give but unwilling to receive. Givers are powerful people. When you give, you are in control, you are strong. When you receive, you are needy.

I saw this illustrated powerfully at a church in an economically impoverished community in Chicago. Each Christmas the church receives dozens of wrapped gifts sent from churches and individuals who want to help. Do you know what this church does? They unwrap the gifts and put them on a shelf for sale to people in the community. They understand that when people simply give something away they can easily destroy the dignity of another. Instead they sell these gifts to people for ten percent of their market value. That way the people of the community can buy gifts for their own children and wrap them themselves and maintain their own dignity.

Jesus could have gotten his own water from the well in Samaria. Since he was traveling, he carried a container for water with him. But there is more to the story. He was teaching something about God. Jesus lifted this woman's worth as a child of God and gave her dignity.

Second, Jesus ignored the barriers. There were several. She was a woman, a Samaritan, an outsider, one who didn't fit in. Jesus acted on purpose to break down the barriers of race and of gender. He didn't stop at the door of this woman's racial and national identity. Many do in this world. Many nations are at war over ethnic strife. A lot of people say that they're not racist, that they don't have anything against people of other races. But their actions prove differently.

Jesus reached across the racial barrier to this different person. He also reached across the barrier of gender, because rabbis would never speak with women in public. He gave her dignity, respect and honor. Christians need to get serious about creating intentional relationships that cross those barriers. Karl Barth said, "The Church exists . . . to set up in the world a new sign which is radically dissimilar to the world's own manner." Jesus did that in breaking down the barriers.

The Samaritan woman's response was one of surprise. "How is it that you, a Jew, ask a drink of me, a woman of Samaria?"

It's like the sign tacked to the rusty screen door of an old back street bar in Piedras Negras, Mexico: "For Members and Nonmembers Only." What an amazing image of God's audience for love: for members and nonmembers only! The barriers we build are barriers that Jesus quickly takes down.

Finally, Jesus called her to the kingdom. In one of John's most remarkable passages the woman says, " 'I know that Messiah is coming.' . . . Jesus said to her, 'I am he, the one who is speaking to you.' "

To this "outsider," this second-class citizen, this one whom religious society considered unworthy, whom political society considered politically incorrect, Jesus revealed his identity as Messiah. To this one Jesus revealed the kingdom! And through her an entire village came to the kingdom. A village responded positively to Jesus despite 150 years of smoldering resentment by Samaritans against the Jews. This woman became the first woman who preached of Jesus outside of Judaism.

Earl Palmer concludes: "What is so profoundly important in the encounter with the Samaritan woman is that she was related to as a unique person who as important as a unique person. She is not lumped into some traditional category but as a human being is honored by the full and individual attention of Jesus Christ" (*The Intimate Gospel*).

God is the Creator of all people. In Jesus God is the Savior of all people. In the church God is the reconciler of all people. Racial reconciliation is not just a politically correct thing to do—it is central to the life of the church. Wherever there are human barriers, Christians need to be the first to build bridges.

Does that mean that Christians condone and accept any behavior, lifestyle or action as valid? Of course not. But Christians must treat others with respect and love in order to bring healing to the world.

A Song of Reconciliation

Laurens Van der Post tells the story of two brothers. The elder was strong, tall, intelligent and an excellent athlete. Sent away to a private school in South Africa, where the family lived, he became an admired leader among the students. His brother was six years younger. He was not good-looking, and he lacked the capabilities of his very competent older brother. Worst of all, due to a birth defect his body was disfigured—he was a hunchback. But he had one great gift. He had a magnificent singing voice.

In time the younger brother was sent off to join his older brother at the boarding school. One day the cruelty of some kids took over, and a group of students attacked the younger brother. They taunted him, mocked him and tore off his shirt to reveal his distorted anatomy. All the while the older brother knew what was happening. He could have gone out and faced the crowd of sadistic students and stopped it from happening. He could have claimed this strange hunchback as his brother and stopped the whole sorry mess. Instead he remained in the chemistry lab completing an assignment. He betrayed his brother by what he failed to do.

The younger brother was never the same again. He returned home to his parents' farm, where he kept to himself and sang no more. The older brother became a soldier and was stationed in Palestine during World War II. One night, lying outdoors and gazing into the starlit sky, he realized what he had done to his younger brother in their school days. His heart told him that he would never have peace until he went home and asked his brother for forgiveness. And so he made the incredibly difficult wartime journey from Palestine to South Africa. The brothers talked long into the night, the elder one confessing his guilt and remorse. They cried together, they embraced, and the breach between them was healed.

But something else happened that night. The older brother had fallen asleep when he was startled awake by the sound of a full, rich, beautiful voice in the night. His younger brother was singing once again.

By one costly, concrete act of contrition and compassionate caring the older brother brought healing and wholeness to his brother, to himself and to the relationship, and beautiful harmony sprang forth into the world—the natural outpouring of the song of reconciliation.

In this brief chapter I can only begin to skim the surface of the issues of reconciliation, racial attitudes and class awareness. I write from the

---

For Black Christians Only

1. Live out the truth of the gospel.
2. Confront racism constructively.
3. Recognize that blacks can have racist attitudes, too.
4. Don't get caught up in bitterness.
5. Avoid the BBW trap (Black people talking to Black people about White people).
6. We need our white brothers and sisters, and they need us.

For White Christians Only

1. Don't deny the reality of racism.
2. Don't look for simple solutions to complex problems.
3. Become a learner by first admitting you don't know very much about black people.
4. Get beyond guilt to action.
5. How much you accomplish depends on how much you invest.
6. White churches must become part of the solution.

Taken from *Breaking Down Walls: A Model for Reconciliation* by Raleigh Washington and Glen Kehrein.

---

limited perspective of a white middle-class male. Two books have been written recently that offer a broader perspective. *More Than Equals* is written by Spencer Perkins, an African-American (son of John Perkins), and Chris Rice, his white coworker and friend. *Breaking Down Walls: A Model for Reconciliation* is by Raleigh Washington and Glen Kehrein. Raleigh is an African-American pastor, and Glenn, a European-American, is executive director of Circle Urban Ministries in Chicago.

The latter two authors say that "intentionality is the locomotive that drives racial reconciliation. It must become part of our attitude. We must want to know the other race, to contribute to the other person's spiritual, social, and emotional growth."

May God help us so to live that the kingdom may come and that God's will may be done.

Questions for Groups

1. Who are the "Samaritans" in your college or university?

2. Create a group definition of *reconciliation*.

What key factors are involved in reconciliation? Is reconciliation different from tolerance? How?

3. What new insights do you have about racial or other prejudice in yourself?

What can you do to be a reconciler for people who live with barriers between them?

4. Pray with thanksgiving for the great reconciler, Jesus Christ.

18

Wake Up, Virginia

About a year ago my daughter Keri, my wife and I attended a Billy Joel concert. It was a fun evening listening to someone whose music I've known for a long time. The four teenage girls in front of us thoroughly enjoyed it as well. When Billy Joel played one song in particular they went crazy, dancing and singing along with sheer delight. The song was one of his early ones, "Only the Good Die Young." In it he sings to Virginia, a young Catholic girl, and tells her to wake up and quit hiding behind the stained-glass windows of the church and its obsolete teachings about sex. His message is clear: Gratuitous, free, unconstrained sexual expression is the norm. To put limits or boundaries on sex is the new taboo. Sex is your right!

The message is: Wake up, Virginia, get on with it—you're old enough to have sex, so go for it. Wake up, Virginia, don't believe that old biblical stuff—what does the Bible know about sex, anyway? Wake up, Virginia, virginity is a thing of the past, to abstain is stupid—you're naive if you think it's better to wait. Sexual experience makes you more of a woman today! You know you'll find the greatest sexual satisfaction if you are more sexually experienced. Wake up, Virginia, sexual expression is your right. Don't let anybody tell you what to do—it's your body.

Wake up, Virginia, love is something you give away, not something you keep, so giving sexual love must be the highest form of love—even if you give it away to various people at different times. Wake up, Virginia, you need to have sex now in order to know if you can really love this guy. Wake up, Virginia, it's got to happen sometime—love, purity and commitment don't have anything to do with it. "I might as well be the one."

But Billy Joel is forgetting a couple of important things.

God Has a Better Idea!

God is the Creator of sex. Doesn't it make more sense to listen to the One who invented the thing more than the guy down the street who is in the middle of a hormone surge? God just might have some good reasons for putting some limits around his creation. Like any great power, sex can be beautiful or horrible, useful or harmful, positive or negative. "Sex is a natural force like fire; and like fire it can weld or warm or it can destroy."

After ten years of working with college students who listened to the popular sexual views of their day, I can tell you stories of people whose worlds have collapsed into terrible pain and trauma because of irresponsible sex. One student had a nervous breakdown after her second abortion—not because of the abortion, but because the guy she "knew" loved her enough to take her to bed was now having sex with one of her best friends! Other students made the painful choice to give up a baby for adoption. Two eighteen-year-olds who had only known each other for the first six weeks of the semester were forced to marry because of a pregnancy. Numerous women dropped out of college and gave up their dreams. Many students secretly, silently suffered with their shame and guilt, telling no one, hiding the truth until finally it could no longer be kept a secret. The songs never quite get around to telling you about the hurt that can follow.

So wake up, Virginia, and take a look at a biblical view of sex. The Bible takes an honest approach to the topic of human sexuality. It doesn't play games—it tells the truth, even if the truth is what people don't like to hear. Paul wrote 1 Thessalonians to Christians, and in the fourth chapter addresses those who desire to be in the will of God in the area of sex. He has four lessons for his readers.

God Values Sex

First, Paul teaches believers to value sex as highly as God does. "It is God's will that you should be sanctified: that you should avoid sexual immorality; that each of you should learn to control his own body in a way that is holy and honorable" (1 Thess 4:3-4 NIV). Many who read that verse see only the injunction against sexual immorality. This may result in the notion that God's view of sex is negative, that it is a long list of don'ts. But there is more here than that. Paul is saying something dramatic. He is telling Christians to value sex as highly as God does. He says that holiness has to do with human sexual behavior. I am amazed at how often that is overlooked.

I have some really good news for you: enjoying sex is not outside of the will of God! The creation account (Gen 1:27-28; 2:24-25) explains that God created sex and that it was created to be something good. All of the work of God's creating was punctuated with that supreme affirmation "It is good."

The first two commandments from God are "have sex and get a good job!" That may be overstated, but not much. First God says, "Be fruitful and multiply." He intends for the human family to be sexual and to procreate. And second: "Fill the earth and subdue it, and have dominion over [it]." God intends for the human family to be caretakers over the earth.

Human bodies are the handiwork of God and can be accepted as part of our giftedness. If the human body were evil in itself, would God have sent his Son Jesus Christ in human flesh, in a fully human body? We act as though we had just discovered human sexuality. We assume that our way of dealing with sex is the most advanced approach yet. The fact is, sex has been around for a long time. Each person has been created as a sexual person.

God Values People

The apostle Paul also teaches his readers to value people as highly as God does. "Each of you should learn to control his own body in a way that is holy and honorable, not in passionate lust like the heathen, who do not know God" (1 Thess 4:4-5 NIV).

Christians are to control their own passions. They are to gain mastery over their own bodies. As Paul defines it, immorality is all sexual intercourse other than that which takes place within the marriage relationship. The radical viewpoint of the Christian Scriptures is that sex outside of marriage is sin. It is sin because it doesn't value people highly enough. It takes work and committed love to relate in totality to another human being. It is easier by far just to relate as body to body and passion to passion, rather than as person to person. No one deserves the dehumanization of sex without love.

A growing number of Christian college students are telling me they can do anything sexually as long as they don't complete the act of sexual intercourse. In other words, any sexual acts short of penetration are OK. Oral sex isn't really the same as having sex. Complete nudity is OK as long as you don't go all the way. This view seems to be exclusive to Christian students; I've never heard non-Christians say that these acts are not "sex."

My response to that viewpoint is this: Don't buy the lie. If you're going to be sexually active, then, like all the other important decisions, you'll make your choice, but please don't lie to yourself that what you're doing is living in holiness. Don't lie to yourself that you're living within God's will just because you don't complete the act of intercourse.

If your goal is to see how far you can go before you're out of God's will, then you have missed the point. God intends that you seek the very best good for the other person. God intends that you do what will build them up in faith and good works for the sake of the kingdom.

God Values Relationships
Paul's third message is to value relationships as highly as God does. "In this matter no one should wrong his brother or take advantage of him. The Lord will punish men for all such sins, as we have already told you and warned you" (1 Thess 4:6 NIV). Paul recognizes that one can wrong

or take advantage of a brother or a sister. The problem in the first-century world was that there was a double standard for the two genders that was taken for granted. Married men had sexual freedom that was not granted to married women. The general attitude is frequently illustrated by a quotation from Demosthenes: "We keep mistresses for pleasure, concubines for our day-to-day bodily needs, but we have wives to produce legitimate children and serve as trustworthy guardians of our homes."

Paul argued instead that relationships are to be highly valued. Echoing the teaching of his Master, Paul elevated the role and place of women; he clearly taught the sanctity of marriage and a warm and encouraging reverence for the family. He called Christians to be models of integrity in their relationships. Society needs that model because it seems to believe that you should get all you can from relationships without paying the price of commitment.

Scripture teaches that love forbids certain attitudes and acts. Love says that some things are clearly wrong. Relationships are important to God, and a casual attitude toward them is not part of God's intentions. Where things are wrong, the Christian attitude is not moderation but abstention.

In the October 17, 1994, edition of *Newsweek*, an article entitled "Virgin Cool" reports with some surprise that virginity is back in fashion again. "A lot of kids are putting off sex, and not because they can't get a date. They've decided to wait, and they're proud of their chastity, not embarrassed by it. Suddenly virgin geek is giving way to virgin chic." The motivations are obviously not biblical or religious, but the result is the same. Students are reclaiming the right to say no. Instead of the attitude of some students twenty years ago—"It's my body and I'll sleep with as many people as I want to"—some are now prepared to say, "It's my body and I don't have to sleep with anyone if I don't want to." So the culture has rediscovered abstinence as a more human value. "Save sex, not 'safe sex'" is today's motto.

One of the very positive characteristics of Generation X is the high value placed on relationships and the renewed emphasis on commitment. Some in the youth culture have seen what their parents and older siblings have missed: sex is not an adequate basis for every male-female relationship. As one student wisely understands it, "If your relationship is based on sex, you don't *have* a relationship." Rather, sex becomes a force that drives people apart or opens the door for unhealthy relationships.

Sex before marriage harms your relationship with the one you will marry. Sex outside of marriage harms your relationship with the person to whom you are married. I wish I could tell you how many times I have seen couples play their own version of roommate roulette. They "fall in love" and become sexually active, only later in the year to fall out of love and then to switch partners with a roommate or a close friend. Are you ready to look that former sexual partner in the eye when you stand at her wedding to someone else?

Sexual intercourse is intended to be a deeply felt, profoundly given gift of one's total self to another person. Exclusively. If God gave that as a guideline, do you think it works better to ignore the instruction manual?

God Values Love

Finally, Paul teaches us to value love as highly as God does. "Now about brotherly love we do not need to write to you, for you yourselves have been taught by God to love each other. . . . Yet we urge you, brothers, to do so more and more" (1 Thess 4:9-10 NIV). In the last few years I've encountered a new concept, something called *secondary virginity*. By itself the term is a contradiction and sounds like a deception you tell yourself. But I remember one college couple who came to see me after their sexual activity got them into deep emotional pain and difficulty. They discovered that sex was their only way of communicating. They were sexually more competent, they knew more about each other physically, but they had stopped growing together. They learned that sex isn't a guarantee of growth. It is easy for two bodies to have sexual intercourse. It doesn't take a lot of intimacy, love or care for the other person.

But this couple wanted something more. So we began to talk, and I challenged them to secondary virginity. I challenged them to abstain from sex until they were married. With great discipline and sometimes great difficulty they did just that. I saw them a few months after the wedding, and they told me that they had approached the marriage and their wedding night as they had intended long ago. It was a new experience of love, respect, trust and holiness. They were no longer virgins in a physical sense, but in an important spiritual sense, they knew what their love was built on.

If you can't control yourself sexually before you get married, what makes you think you'll be able to later? What makes you think you can trust yourself or your partner later?

Making Choices

I want to end this chapter with several words to specific people.

To those who have been faithful to your intentions to sexual purity: keep up the good fight; it is worth it.

To those who have been badly abused by previous sexual activity: there is healing in the all-pervasive love of God.

To those who have crossed the line and desire to step back again: it can be done, and I pray that you will find the love of our all-forgiving God.

To those who have simply chosen the way of sexual activity and have no intentions of stopping: I pray that God will soften your hearts to seek the holiness of life that Jesus intends for you. I'd especially like you to consider some key questions about the choice you've made.

Does this sexual activity make your relationship better? Many people assume that great sex means you have a great relationship, but every year on our campus I see students who have become sexually active break up and find themselves just as lonely, incomplete and frustrated as before. Sexual activity in a relationship is not a guarantee that the relationship will improve. In fact, it often complicates the relationship and causes couples to fail to grow in their communication with one another.

Can your relationship survive for a month without sexual activity? If not, you need to ask yourself, what is the basis for this relationship? Is it truly a love for the other person or a selfish need for personal gratification?

Does sexual activity make you a better person? Be selfish in your thoughts for a moment. Will this sexual activity help you to grow into the kind of person you want to be? Are you able to live by the values that you have chosen and by the convictions that are truly your own? Many people are drawn into sexual promiscuity because they believe it shows maturity and growth. Often it actually shows an immature selfishness and self-preoccupation.

Will this relationship develop you into a stronger follower of Jesus Christ? Everything in our lives should draw us closer to him.

I met together with a group of male students for nearly a year. The trust level was significant, and one day the discussion turned to the inevitable: relationships with women. I asked them the question, "Why do you seek to be chaste, to be faithful to God's teaching about sex as appropriate only in marriage?"

One answer was new to me, but powerful. "The facts of life are that the woman I date today may be the wife of one of these other guys in another year or two. My relationship with them is important to me, and I want a strong and positive relationship with both of them if that happens."

Because relationships in college can be so very temporary, it is helpful to remember that tomorrow she may be your best friend's girlfriend or he may be your best friend's husband. The guys in my group were saying that they need to express loyalty to one another even in advance of marriage.

So wake up, men and women: God has something important to say about one of life's greatest gifts!

Questions for Groups

Begin with an agreement to treat this discussion with special care because of its very personal and sensitive nature. Pray for an ability to be honest and vulnerable to each other in the discussions that lie immediately ahead.

1. What messages about sex and sexuality did you receive as a child? What was the source of information about sex in your background?

2. Create a group definition of "holy sexuality." In other words, create a list of God's goals and purposes for sexuality.

3. How far should you go? This is *the* question for Christian students. As a group, try to create some guidelines that are biblically faithful and practically helpful.
4. Pray for each other as you seek to be faithful to the teaching of God's Word on sexual behavior.

19

The Gay Debate

K risten sat in my office with a pained look on her face. She told me her story, and we talked for a long time. She was raised in a good Christian home. She knew all about Christian views on sexuality, and everything was OK until she met Karen. Her life took a dramatic turn when Karen, her new piano teacher, began to pay her special attention. She started with extra words of praise and affirmation for Kristen's piano accomplishments; then she began to show special affection for Kristen. From there it became physical. And then Karen admitted aloud to Kristen, "I feel strong attraction to you." It scared Kristen, but it also struck a chord deep within her and raised some very hard questions for her life. "What am I supposed to think about homosexuality?" she asked. "And what am I supposed to do about Karen?"

There is probably no more divisive issue in the church today than homosexuality. The very mention of the word can stir such deep, immediate emotional responses that many people are immobilized from any further rational listening after that.

You can respond in several different ways to the controversy and the delicate issue of homosexuality. You can do what the church has done for centuries—ignore it. You can bury your head in the sand and ignore the public debates, social changes and legislative action on behalf of the gay and lesbian community. Or you can lash out in anger and condemnation against homosexuals. You can label "them" all as perverts and degenerates and distance yourself from them all. Or you can be afraid. You can be afraid for the future of the nation, afraid for children, defensively lashing out because of your fear and ignorance. Or you can be confused. You can simply choose to remain in the dark and ignore new information, new understandings and new insights. Finally, you can do what some argue for today: completely reverse centuries of thinking and condone homosexuality as a legitimate, God-approved way of life.

One of the problem areas in the debate about homosexuality is the difficulty in defining it. In *Eros Defiled* the Christian psychiatrist John White gives one of the clearest definitions I have heard. He writes that "a homosexual act is one designed to produce sexual orgasm between members of the same sex. A homosexual is a man or woman who engages in homosexual acts." The emphasis is thus on behavior and acts rather than on personalities or lifestyles. Gary Collins, a Christian psychologist, points out that there are several forms of homosexuality. Overt homosexuals are those who regularly engage in overt homosexual acts. Latent homosexuals have what is called a "same-sex" attraction, but they do not act on it. Circumstantial homosexuals are those who temporarily choose homosexual behavior because opposite-sex partners are not available (some prisoners fall into this category).

What causes homosexuality? There is no universally accepted, clearly identified single cause. Some have argued that it is the result of physiological and biological problems. But studies of physical build, chromosomes, neurological and biochemical makeup and even hormones have failed to show significant differences between homosexuals and heterosexuals. That leads some to argue that it is a learned behavior. Others say that it is caused by parent-child relationships—specifically occurring in children who have a weak, passive father and a domineering mother. The son loses confidence in his masculinity and dreads the thought of intimacy with women. The daughter sees her father as rejecting and unfriendly and finds that she relates better to women. Others attribute it to a family where there were no clear male/female role models for the child, or where there was a fearful silence regarding sexual matters, or an overindulgence of the child. Still others say that it is caused by fear, from a lack of male or female contact during a child's formative years. And some will argue that it is strictly a matter of willful choice, of a lifestyle preference.

Homosexuality is a complex issue. I find that I cannot take the simplistic approach of "Dear Abby." A woman wrote to her and said that she had "two daughters, one heterosexual and one a lesbian," and asked, "Where did I fail?" Abby replied: "You haven't failed. One daughter is straight. The other is gay. One thing is certain. God made gays just as surely as he made straights and all His children are entitled to love and [to] be loved in dignity. Remember, we are all family." In a single paragraph she answers too easily centuries of questions with theological, ethical and psychological implications. However, she does make one important statement: all of God's children *are* entitled to love and to be loved in dignity.

The Bible and Homosexuality

Christians find their ethical considerations and, I would hope, their lifestyle considerations based in the study of Scripture. But the Scriptures have relatively little to say directly about homosexuality. Seven passages mention it briefly. What I found surprising in my own study is that these texts are not as simple and clear-cut as I had previously believed. The complex questions must be answered text by text.

The Old Testament is not as direct and clear as we might suppose. Some scholars argue that it condemns all homosexuality. Others argue that it condemns homosexual acts only under the ritual, ceremonial law that was put aside when Christ came to die for our sins. Leviticus 18:22—"Do not lie with a man as one lies with a woman; that is detestable"—is one such passage. It is part of the ceremonial law, which also includes such rules as "Do not plant your fields with two kinds of seeds."

The New Testament, on the other hand, is clear in its treatment of homosexuality. It condemns overt homosexuality in several passages, along with idolatry, thievery, lying and other sins. Nothing is said, however, about homosexual thoughts or temptations. Are they sin too?

Genesis is the starting point for a biblical understanding of sexuality in general and of homosexuality in particular. The aim of Christian sexuality is not personal satisfaction but interpersonal completeness. "For this reason a man will leave his father and mother and be united to his wife, and they will become one flesh" (Gen 2:24 NIV); " 'for this reason a man will leave his father and mother and be united to his wife, and the two will become one flesh.' So they are no longer two, but one" (Mt 19:5-6 NIV).

The biblical prescription is this: one plus one equals one, completeness. This is a mystery, but it is also clear, I believe. The ideal is one of completeness based on the coming together of differences. These differences are not just genital but of personality, temperament, social function and so forth. In *The Sacramentality of Sex* John W. Dixon concludes, "[Homosexuality] is not a valid model of sexuality, for it affirms incompleteness. . . . In sexual matters, fulfillment is completeness, the coming together of differences." In the creation process, God declared the very purpose of human sexuality and gave us the valid human model of sexuality: "So God created humankind in his image, in the image of God he created them; male and female he created them" (Gen 1:27).

Let's Get to the Point

What can we learn about homosexuality from all of this?

Biblically speaking, it must be said that homosexuality at the very least represents a state of human incompleteness. It is not just a valid alternative way of living life. Two men cannot become "one flesh"; two women cannot become "one flesh." The homosexual lifestyle expresses a basic rejection of God's design for humanity. One writer said, "The very biology attests to the theological mystery: I, a man, am made for the other; but not just any other. I am made for the other who is also the image of God, but not me. Nor a mirror image of myself." Homosexuality, then, is certainly not God's design for the entire human family.

Second, homosexual feelings are normal in a child's development. One must recognize that fact and not be afraid of them or overreact to them. There is curiosity about one's own sexual identity, which often leads to sexual feelings of all kinds in children and adolescents. These feelings may even lead them to touch one another or to acts some might label "homosexual." Don't jump too quickly to attach that label to a child or a young person who has these feelings or has had an experience that might even be labeled homosexual.

Third, the adult practice of homosexual behavior is sin and needs to be seen as sin. Romans 1:24-27 is not simply a cultural statement of Paul's. It is a theological statement teaching that historically, people have exchanged God's best for a second best, exchanging God's truth about who they are for a lie about who they are. Sin is an act of rebellion against God's design, transgressing God's laws or his plans. It is missing the mark of his intentions. It is choosing a lesser choice than his choice for us.

Finally, though, homosexuality is not the unforgivable sin. It is not the "worst" of the sins—in fact, I find little to support any ranking of sins or hierarchy of sins. Romans 3:23 says that there are no distinctions, for "all have sinned and fall short of the glory of God."

The Stranger Within the Gates

I asked a couple of students if I should include a chapter on homosexuality in this book. Their answer was swift: "Yes! We know what we've been told about it, but we still have questions about how to relate to friends who are gay. Does Christianity have any help to give us on that?"

Several years ago I interviewed an AIDS patient for a collegewide symposium. When it was announced that this man would attend the symposium, letters and calls poured in from worried and irate parents. "You cannot expose my son to that homosexual!" "I will not tolerate you forcing my daughter to be in the same room with someone with AIDS." In the end we decided to save the AIDS patient the potential outrage and abuse from students, so I videotaped the interview in advance.

When he walked into the studio I found myself facing all of my own fears and questions about AIDS. He approached me, but didn't hold out his hand until I reached forward to greet him and to welcome him.

114

I'll admit that I had thought about that simple step for some time before he arrived. But I did what I believe Jesus would do when I welcomed him and offered him hospitality.

A terrifying attitude of judgmentalism and condemnation runs rampant in the church today, especially in the conservative and evangelical church. One writer calls it the shameful scandal of homophobia and the rejection of homosexuals. But in Matthew 25 Jesus deliberately and intentionally identified himself with those who were hungry and thirsty, who were strangers and prisoners, who were the outcasts. He took literally the Old Testament teachings that one should treat others with hospitality and welcome the stranger within the gate (Lev 19:33-34).

Hebrews 13:2 instructs Christians to show hospitality to strangers because they may be messengers (angels) in our midst. Hospitality is what one offers the stranger within the gate, even if that stranger has a lifestyle that you do not condone. Hospitality means to create a free and open space where people can meet one another. Its opposite is hostility, a fearful reaction against the stranger. One should offer hospitality to all people.

Do you condone the lifestyle, the abuses and the gay/lesbian agenda by such hospitality? I think not. Jesus did not condone the behavior of some people he met, but he loved them all. He taught his followers to love even those they consider to be enemies, and he warned them not to judge or condemn, lest they be judged and condemned likewise. Rather, Jesus offers a formula for the treatment of those with whom one disagrees most strongly: "Be merciful, just as your Father is merciful" (Lk 6:36). Some translate this verse "Be compassionate because God is compassionate." These teachings do not allow for the moral absolutism of many in the church today. Neither do they allow a tolerance for the cult of absolute relativism that rules the philosophy of the day.

At a baccalaureate service, my colleague Daniel Taylor finished his prayer with a powerful word for our graduates: "Be as tolerant as God, but not more so." There are limits to tolerance. Compassion for all is required of the Christian, but compassion does not mean endorsement. Christians need to recognize that homosexuality is a deviation from the norm of God's will in creating us male and female. Each person is responsible before God for the choices made—for what one chooses to do with the gift of life.

If you or someone you care about is dealing with the problem of homosexuality, remember that the Bible's message, Jesus' gospel, is the announcement of good news, of wholeness, of healing, hope and change. Not one person has arrived at maturity in all areas of life. Everyone needs growth—sexual, intellectual, relational, moral. Everyone is on a pilgrimage of growth. If this is an area in which you battle, talk about it and seek resources for help.

I have left much unsaid. I have given some background, some statements on causes, some sketches of the biblical positions and of the complexities involved. My hope is that this discussion opens conversation and dialogue within your community of Christians. The questions Kristen raised weren't answered in one simple, easy conversation but took an ongoing relationship with her, many continuing conversations and prayer.

Questions for Groups

Remember to pray again for sensitivity and compassion as you discuss this divisive topic.

1. What did your family and church teach you about homosexuality?

2. Look up the seven biblical texts that refer directly to homosexuality: Genesis 19:1-11, Leviticus 18:22, 20:13, Judges 19:22-25, Romans 1:26-27, 1 Corinthians 6:9, 1 Timothy 1:9-10.

3. Discuss this as a hypothetical situation: Your best friend has just told you that he/she is a homosexual. Based on your understanding of Scripture and the discussion in this chapter, what would you say and do?

4. Identify where you need to grow personally in your attitudes, understanding and reactions toward homosexuals.

20

Lonely People

Nathan sat in my office with an embarrassed look on his face. "I don't know how you'll take this," he said, "but I find myself almost paralyzed because of my loneliness. My motivation to try new friendships is gone. My interest in old friendships is gone. I feel depressed. I feel alone. I don't know for sure that a single person on the earth cares whether I live or die."

Nathan felt what countless other students feel every day: the nagging ache of loneliness. College students need a sense of belonging or affiliation. As one comic said, "Loneliness wouldn't be so hard to fight if I didn't have to do it all by myself." Loneliness. Even in the midst of a busy residence hall. Even with all of the activity swirling around students on campus. Even for Christians surrounded by fellowship groups, Bible studies, mission teams and outreach groups. Loneliness. The feeling that I am here but no one notices or cares. The feeling that I just do not matter to others. The feeling that everyone around me has what I want most—friends to whom I matter, acceptance and appreciation. Loneliness can be a painful and horrible experience.

Melinda felt the extreme loneliness that many first-year students feel. "I wish there was someone I could call in the middle of the night and know they would answer, someone who cares, someone who would say, 'I'm there 100 percent for you.' "

Where Does Loneliness Come From?

There are several kinds of loneliness. Social isolation or social loneliness comes when a person is cut off from a network of family and friends for a period of time. It comes from leaving everything that is known and familiar. Emotional isolation may come when a significant relationship is taken away, for whatever reason. Some even speak of a kind of loneliness called existential loneliness, where a person's life lacks value or meaning. This person feels alienated from God.

An elderly widow once wrote a letter to the newspaper and said, "I see no human beings. My phone never rings. I feel sure the world has ended. I'm the only one on earth. How else can I feel? All alone. They say, 'pay your rent and go back to your room.' I'm so lonely I don't know what to do." She enclosed six stamps with her letter and said, "Will someone write me, anyone?"

Our society is filled with lonely people. Some believe that loneliness is the greatest problem confronting teenagers today. Those whose lives have been complicated by the loss of a parent or through a change in family lifestyle experience loneliness most keenly. However, any experience of loss can create loneliness.

A class of twelve- and thirteen-year-olds was asked to write sentences describing a feeling. A disproportionately large number wrote about loneliness.

Inside, I look like a big red water balloon. Everybody liked me and played with me and I popped. Nobody plays with me now. Loneliness tastes like cotton candy that melts in your mouth and it doesn't come back. Sadness is gray like an empty world. Loneliness pries into a person, eats up feelings of hope and joy. It leaves depression, sadness and aloneness. You may never reach the top of loneliness, but when you do you will want to get out. It's like you fall and never stop.

A college student told me that loneliness is "like a continual heartache that won't go away."

The causes of loneliness in the larger society are many. One is mobility. I work with a student now who has moved sixteen times in her nineteen years of life! Others blame the urbanization of our world, the fast pace of life and the chronic failure of marriages. These factors create a mistrust of relationships and a pessimism about their success. Also, physical or physiological factors can cause emotional distress, depression and even loneliness.

There is a mistaken idea that you cannot be lonely if you are with other people. If you have a roommate, you cannot be lonely. If you live in a suite with five or six others, you cannot be lonely. If you go to classes with other people, you cannot be lonely. Yet sometimes lonely people feel their loneliness most acutely in the midst of the crowd. Some even believe that you cannot be lonely if you are a Christian. As I said, these are mistaken notions.

Lonely, but Not Alone

Where do lonely people come from? They are born that way. Everyone is thrust into this life knowing loneliness, because God intends it to be that way. Why? Because those feelings drive us, spur us, encourage us, even compel us to seek a solution to that need within. God created us to feel loneliness, but not to be alone. "It is not good that the man should be alone" (Gen 2:18). Henri Nouwen writes,

> The Christian way of life does not take away our loneliness, it protects and cherishes it as a precious gift. Sometimes it seems as if we do everything possible to avoid the painful confrontation with our basic human loneliness, and allow ourselves to be trapped by false gods promising immediate satisfaction and quick relief. But perhaps the painful awareness of loneliness is an invitation to transcend our limitations and look beyond the boundaries of our existence. The awareness of loneliness might be a gift we must protect and guard, because our loneliness reveals to us an inner emptiness that can be destructive when misunderstood, but filled with promise for him who can tolerate its sweet pain.

Loneliness, then, is far from the enemy of being human. Nouwen says it is "the prodder of our souls toward becoming fully human, fully alive. Loneliness is a gift, not a barrier toward our fulfillment." Where do all the lonely people come from? In this sense, they come from God.

But that's an abstract and conceptual notion. What about the practical reality of loneliness on campus? I see it all of the time.

First-year students may slip into it as a kind of homesickness that sets in after a few weeks. You wake to realize that you really live in this place. You are here for the long haul, and you don't really know these people. Or your roommate is gone for the weekend, and you're left alone in the room. It sounded like a great idea on Friday, but by Saturday you begin to feel loneliness creeping in like a heavy fog. All of the homework you intended to do is still there staring back at you, waiting. For most students that kind of encounter with loneliness is short-term, and then they're back to normal. For some, however, loneliness sets in as a regular part of life and sometimes leads to serious depression and even thoughts or acts of suicide.

Generation X has been described by some as a generation of the clinically depressed. Soul Asylum rocks out the words "I am homesick for the home I've never had." For this generation, feelings such as these can be a positive force that drives people into community, into relationships built on trust, acceptance, love and authenticity.

What Can One Lonely Person Do?
First, you need to tell someone how you feel. That person may be a counselor at your campus counseling center, a peer counselor, a professor, your resident assistant or resident director, or your campus pastor. It may be your mother! But telling someone is a good and healthy place to start.

Paul Tournier says this in *To Understand Each Other:*

Listen to all the conversations of our world, those between nations as well as those between couples. They are for the most part dialogues of the deaf. Exceedingly few exchanges of viewpoints manifest a real desire to understand the other person.

No one can find a full life without feeling understood by at least one person. Misunderstood, she loses self-confidence, she loses her faith in life, or even in God. Here is an even greater mystery: no one comes to him or herself through introspection, or in the solitude of his or her personal diary. He who would see himself clearly, she who would see herself clearly must open up to a confidant, freely chosen and worthy of such trust.

Second, you need to tell God how you feel. Whenever I suggest that to students they seem to recoil in fear or shock. "How can I tell God something like that? God might be displeased with me because I don't have it all worked out. Maybe I should get my spiritual life in order first and then I can go to God." I always invite them to look at the most honest book ever written, the book of Psalms. Do these people sound like they have it all together? "Attend to me and answer me; I am troubled in my complaint. . . . My heart is in anguish within me" (Ps 55:2, 4). "Rouse yourself, come to my help and see!" (in other words, wake up God, I need you!) (Ps 59:4). "From the end of the earth I call to you, when my heart is faint" (Ps 61:2).

Save me, O God,
    for the waters have come up to my neck.
I sink in deep mire,
    where there is no foothold;
I have come into deep waters,
    and the flood sweeps over me.
I am weary with my crying;
    my throat is parched.
My eyes grow dim
    with waiting for my God. (Ps 69:1-3)

The psalms were the prayer book of Jesus. He read these words every day and learned to bring everything to God. The people of ancient Israel didn't separate life into compartments but lived everything in relationship to God. They brought their honest complaints to God. Like them, you should bring your laments to God. Tell God what it feels like to be you right now.

Third, remember what you know about God. Call to your memory the character of God. Call to your memory the very nature of God.

In Lamentions the writer begins by speaking of the loneliness of the city. He then talks about the great affliction and pain he has experienced. He even blames God for it and says, "Against me alone he turns his hand, again and again, all day long. . . . Though I call and cry for help, he shuts out my prayer" (3:3, 8).

Then he remembers to remember. "But this I call to mind, and therefore I have hope: The steadfast love of the Lord never ceases, his mercies never come to an end; they are new every morning; great is your faithfulness" (3:21-23). He remembers the character of God as the merciful and loving One. He remembers that God is love. Maybe he remembered some of the biblical characters whose lives ran into hard times. Maybe he thought of Abraham on the road with Sarah, not even sure where they were going.

Fourth, look for ways to serve others. That may sound like sheer craziness, but what have you got to lose? I have watched people climb out of their loneliness and isolation when they reached out to others in need. It may not make sense at the time, especially when you feel like you are the one in greatest need. But something happens in the process of loving and caring for others. The most often repeated comment from students who go out on our outreach and missions teams is "I thought I was going to help serve others, and I got the greatest blessing from it." Great things come from doing the important work of loving others.

Beth agreed grudgingly to go to Tijuana on a missions trip. It would be warmer than Minnesota, she reasoned, but she wasn't prepared for what happened. In the midst of building houses for the poor, she met Dana. She came back with a friendship that has continued for several years.

Fifth, seek the fellowship of the community of faith. If your school has a chapel program, go to chapel and seek out others. If your school has discipleship programs or Bible studies, join them. Part of the work of the Holy Spirit is to be a kind of glue for groups of people.

Jesus knew the pain of loneliness as he died on the cross and faced the isolation from God that caused him to cry out with such anguish, "My God, my God, why have you forsaken me?" When Jesus spoke of his departure he promised the disciples he would not leave them alone. When he sends the Spirit to the church, he sends One who will stand alongside you to bring you into the fellowship of the church.

For some the very act of Eucharist or the Lord's Supper is a strong reminder of our connections to one another. For some the music of faith is a strong reminder that we belong to one another. For some the prayers of others when we ourselves cannot pray are the link to God that we need.

Finally, realize that healing takes time. This is true of emotional healing as well as of physical. Don't expect an overnight fix or an instant cure. No twelve-step program will "cure" your loneliness. What I have given you in this chapter is not a formula but some ideas that have helped me in my own times of loneliness.

Melinda still struggles with loneliness. She hasn't found that one good friend yet. She stops by periodically to tell me how she's coping with things. Next fall she's going to move into a townhouse with five other women students whom she's just getting to know. She's hopeful.

Questions for Groups

1. If you are able, share an experience of loneliness with the group.

2. Do you agree with Nouwen that loneliness can be valuable and productive?

3. What brings help to people who are lonely? What have you experienced that was helpful to your own experience of loneliness?

4. Ask each member of the group how you can pray for them in this area of their life right now.

21

Stress and a Grasshopper Named Norman

*O*ne year just before spring break, I felt weary, worn out, demoralized, stressed and stretched by the events of the early weeks of the semester, as well as by the normal craziness of life in the office of campus ministries. During break, instead of relaxing and working at reducing stress, I went on a mission trip to Tijuana with about twenty college students. Something happened to me on that trip that was very important. I remembered something precious.

Perhaps it was the dramatic contrast to my world of light switches, coffee makers and refrigeration. Perhaps it was the pace of life where people are valued before productivity and output. Perhaps it was seeing students actually surviving without hair blowers, curling irons and designer clothing. Whatever it was, I remembered something and was transformed by it.

I remembered why I got into this business in the first place. I remembered that I am a believer, a true believer in a gospel message that brings love, reconciliation and dignity to all persons through the saving life and death of Jesus Christ. I remembered that to hoard your spirituality violates who you are as a human person, because you are created to love and to give, and if you don't give away what God gives you, you will become a sick person.

I also was *re-membered* by my time with the students. That is, I became a member again of a community of people in a fresh, unique way. I made connections and became part of a community that is also essential to our life. We are part of one another.

Tijuana got me centered again in what I do. As I used a hammer to put shingles on a roof, I realized (again) the sacredness of my actions. I recognized (again) that everything and anything can hold the sacred. It returned me to the joy that was mine before.

Norman the Grasshopper

Once upon a time there was this grasshopper named Norman. He was not your ordinary run-of-the-field grasshopper, you understand, but a real ambitious fellow and a regular guy. Early in his life Norman set out to become the strongest grasshopper in the world. So while his friends ate dandelion leaves and hopped grass all day, Norman lifted weights and rode an exercise cycle. He began on a small scale by lifting twigs and ten-penny nails and things like that and learning to breathe from the diaphragm. Later he progressed to small stones and croquet balls. He took to giving exhibitions for the other insects under a large cabbage leaf (at cost, of course) and even added a dance number and told jokes about his mother-in-law.

Everybody was impressed. After all, it's not every day you see a grasshopper pick up truck tires and anvils. His fame spread.

His agent (a really sharp tumble bug from Des Moines) landed him a spot at Madison Square Garden. Excitement was in the air on opening night. Norman was confident as he ran through his warmups. It was glorious! This was even better than professional wrestling.

Norman planned to lift a Steinway baby grand piano as his finale. So amid oohs and ahhs and assorted gasps, he hefted the most weight of his life by balancing the piano just under middle C. Unfortunately his foot slipped and . . . well, you can figure out what happened!

The moral of the story is, there comes a point when grand ideas become a burden. A person's faith can become a weight instead of a joy.

It's Getting Close to Crunch Time

Some of that happens partway through the semester for many students.

You reach the middle of a semester or quarter and find that the enthusiasm of September has now gone south. I hear it all of the time: "It's getting close to crunch time. We're not quite to finals week, but reality has set in because I finally opened the syllabus and figured out that I have three exams in the same week and a paper due on Friday."

Jen was hitting burnout. She was a resident assistant, on student senate, in the college choir, carrying nineteen credits and working fifteen hours a week. She had no time with her roommates, and her boyfriend had practically forgotten her name. She wasn't close to crunch time, she was past it. Stress was her middle name!

Stress is how a rubber band feels when it is stretched beyond its intended size. Stress is what you feel when you too are stretched and then discover there's still another professor who has expectations for your time. I know that some stress is good—it causes growth. Some stress, however, creates the panic attack! There is not enough time to do everything you need to do. What can you do about the stress you feel in the middle of the semester?

First, remember what this feels like. Why? Because it will come again next semester. If you can remember it earlier, you can plan your schedule with care. Think about your planning when you're in the middle of crunch time, not during semester break when you're sitting by the pool in Malibu.

Sometimes you may get caught up in cycles or patterns of self-destructive habits that contribute to your stress level. You may not plan your homework schedule well. You may not develop good sleep patterns.

I recently asked my 8:30 a.m. class to tell me what time they went to bed the night before. (My keen eye had picked up the chronic sleepiness in class of several students.) Only one guy had been to bed before midnight, and he was married! Five or six had gone to bed at about 1:00 a.m. The rest went to bed no earlier than 2:00. Is it any wonder they were sleepy at 8:30 a.m.?

Unhealthy eating patterns can also create physical stress or distress. At 7:30 a.m. a student walked in with her ever-present can of Mountain Dew, popular among students because of its high caffeine level. "I start every morning with Mountain Dew for breakfast." Not exactly what the doctor ordered for the healthy way to start your day!

Second, keep it all in perspective. You can rarely do your best. I am serious. Remember Jen? How could she do her best in every one of those situations? You may not be able to do your very best, but always do your best *given your circumstances*. If your computer loses a fifteen-page paper and you only have three hours to turn it in, your "best" won't be your very best ever. If you get the flu in the middle of finals week, your best is moderated by your physical condition.

A regular program for physical exercise is an important part of your academic life. It keeps you healthy. It provides a feeling of relaxation and release of tensions that comes in no other way.

Further, all of the literature on stress reduction agrees: it is imperative that you cultivate positive attitudes through setting realistic goals. It's a way of fulfilling recognized needs.

Third, keep your eyes on the prize! That's Paul's advice. Keep your eyes on the target you've set for yourself. It will help to keep the motivation high during crunch times.

Martin Luther King Jr. told a story about himself during the hard days of the Montgomery bus protest. Describing one night when he was at the end of his rope, physically and mentally, he said, "I was about to give up. . . . My head in my hands, I bowed over the kitchen table and prayed aloud. The words I spoke to God that night are vivid in my memory. 'I am here taking a stand for what I believe is right. But now I am afraid. I am at the end of my powers. I have nothing left.'" King continued, "At that moment I experienced the presence of the divine as I had never experienced him. It seemed as though I could hear the quiet assurance of an inner voice saying, 'Stand up for righteousness, stand up for truth. And lo I will be with you, even unto the end of the world.' . . . I heard the voice of Jesus saying still to fight on. He promised never to leave me, never to leave me alone." Further, he wrote, "Almost at once my fears began to go. My uncertainty disappeared" (quoted in David Garrow, *Bearing the Cross*).

God is faithful. He was faithful to Abraham, whom he called to a new place. He was faithful to Moses, whom he called to lead his people out of Egypt. He was faithful to Gideon, David, Samuel, Deborah, Elijah. And to you and to me.

Sometimes in the middle of a school year, you need to hear the words of Paul from Eugene Peterson's wonderful translation of the Bible, *The Message:* "There has never been the slightest doubt in my mind that the God who started this great work in you would keep at it and bring it to a flourishing finish on the very day Jesus Christ appears."

Questions for Groups
1. Talk about how the school year is going for you.
2. What are the highs of the year for you? What are the current lows?
3. Identify for each other the areas that need to be reoriented in your lives.
4. Take a longer time to pray. Take time to get still and to wait for God. Listen carefully and ask in prayer: Where is my life in need of refreshing right now? Ask God to bring you that refreshment and to empower you to complete the tasks that lie ahead.

22

Take This Job and Love It

One of my favorite cartoons shows a guy standing in front of his parents, decked out in cap and gown. He holds the coveted diploma in his hand—that piece of paper you are seeking with such energy. His father asks the question that most of you have been asked at least once in your life: "Well, son, now what do you want to be when you grow up?"

The son looks at his father, looks at his mother, looks at his diploma, then looks at the floor sheepishly and says, "Well, Dad, I still want to be a cowboy."

Not exactly the response his father had in mind, I'm sure, but it's a great question, one that you will ask yourself at numerous points in your life.

A few students arrive at college certain of their goals. Stacy probably knew she wanted to be a nurse when she was four years old, and she hasn't deviated from that plan even for a minute. Jessi, on the other hand, struggles to make "the big decision." She cringes every time someone asks the question and uses the M word: "What is your major?" She doesn't know.

Jessi and I talked about careers, jobs and decision-making. One thing I told her is to get rid of the myth of the single career choice. Some estimate today that a person changes jobs five times in their lifetime. I did it dozens of times as a child before I even started working.

I most remember three aspirations: attorney, radio broadcaster and college professor. I thought about playing third base for the Cubs for a while, but my .203 batting average in Little League caused me to drop that idea.

I also told Jessi that it's OK to be undecided as a first-year student in the second month of school. And then we opened up the New Testament and talked about "vocations." Colossians 3:22-25 contains some powerful principles about work, vocation and jobs. It begins with one big idea: our work is an opportunity to serve Jesus Christ. This is true for two reasons. To begin with, all of life is sacred. As one writer explains it, "As Christians your motive in everything you do is to serve Jesus Christ—you are not the kind of worker who needs constant supervision to *force* you to do your work well—your labor is not done to satisfy a human boss, but everything you do is intended for the approval of our Lord."

Verse 23 expands that thought to its outer limits: whatever you do—do it for the Lord. This may not help you make "the big decision" and settle the questions about a major, a career and the rest of your life, but it reminds you of one huge truth: God is interested in your motives. God cares about your intentions and your heart every bit as much as he cares about your major and your career. Your motive is to serve Jesus Christ. Some of you may be saying, "But you've never worked where I do; the Lord wouldn't even dare to go into that place." No matter: whatever you do—do it for the Lord. "You're not hearing me. I work with some pretty coarse people in a pretty meaningless job." No matter: whatever you do—do it for the Lord.

Remember the context and audience of this passage. Paul is writing specifically to Christian slaves. Their "whatever" might be exceedingly menial and meaningless, but Paul says that when it is done for Christ, it takes on new significance. Your work is an opportunity to serve Jesus Christ because all of life is sacred. Your job is your opportunity to act out a living litany every day. There are not compartments of life called "sacred," "time to serve Jesus" and "job"—only "time to serve Jesus." Perhaps it is in our jobs that we must learn most about serving the Lord. For the church focuses endlessly on prayer, worship, missions and other "religious" activities, but most of you will spend forty or fifty or sixty hours a week in a secular setting doing "secular work," unless you see it through kingdom eyes.

Be a Brain Surgeon

Chaim Potok wanted to be a writer from an early age, but when he went to college his mother took him aside and said, "Chaim, I know you want to be a writer, but I have a better idea. Why don't you be a brain surgeon. You'll keep a lot of people from dying; you'll make a lot of money."

Chaim replied, "No, mama. I want to be a writer."

This conversation was repeated every vacation break, every summer, every meeting: "Chaim, I know you want to be a writer, but listen to your mama. Be a brain surgeon. You'll keep a lot of people from dying; you'll make a lot of money."

Each time Chaim relied, "No, mama. I want to be a writer."

The pressure intensified until finally his mother exploded: "Chaim, you're wasting your time. Be a brain surgeon. You'll keep a lot of people from dying; you'll make a lot of money."

And he said, "Mama, I don't want to keep people from dying; I want to show them how to live!" (As quoted by Eugene Peterson in *Under the Unpredictable Plant.*)

We are called, every one of us, to do that: to show others how to live.

I recently read a book that included the line "Find the job you love to do and you'll never have to work a day in your life." There's a ring of nice sentiment about that. I think I understand it and may even agree with it, but I believe that Christian faith says something slightly different: "Find a God who loves you, and you'll never be without something significant to do with your life."

If you understand that your life is lived for Jesus Christ, your life, especially your work life, can be transformed. Endless hours, great energy and continuous thought are spent choosing a major and a career. All of that is important, maybe even necessary. But all of those issues are step two. Step one is to understand your vocation, your calling, to understand whom you serve. You are called first not to a job but to a relationship with God. Out of that relationship comes the job.

So get first things first. Each person is given a calling. In fact, Christians share a common calling. As Ben Patterson puts it, there is "one vocation, many occupations."

Your calling may well be a calling to business, accounting, nursing, research, administration, engineering, sales, marketing or parenting. But your Christian calling is to see that work is your opportunity for service for Jesus Christ. You may not even get a job that utilizes your skills or education. Job availability is lower in society today, and many students are working well below their ability level. This makes Paul's teachings even more sharply pointed than before.

Your work is an opportunity to serve Jesus Christ, because all of life is sacred, and because meaning is found in Jesus Christ.

In his book *Work*, Studs Terkel, that great observer of American life, quotes a man who said, "I think most of us are looking for a calling, not a job. . . . Jobs are not big enough for people." But as I think back on people I have known, I see people caught up in jobs.

Too many people use jobs to "make a living" instead of finding their meaning in a calling given to them for kingdom reasons. The purpose of their work is to make money to do something else. Work done for the sake of getting money alone is poverty-stricken when it comes to meaning. This kind of work will leave you drained, exhausted, burned out and depleted where it really counts—in the human spirit. Meaning like that comes only when you commit yourself to a larger purpose.

Where There's a Why There's a Way

Viktor Frankl was an Austrian psychiatrist who survived the concentration camps of Germany. He was convinced that the need to find meaning in life is essential to humankind. He observed the harsh brutalities of the camps, the long hours of work, poor shelter, insufficient sleep, terrible food. But as the months wore on he isolated a pattern: those who had something to live for survived, whether it was family, a girlfriend, a child, a business, a dream. Frankl concluded that when people have a "why" they can cope with the "hows" of life. If I have a why, I can discover meaning in what I do. If I have no why on which to hang my life, everything dissolves into despair. Paul says that serving Jesus Christ gives our lives meaning.

I am not saying that all work will be satisfying, fulfilling and enjoyable. Some work has to be done just to keep wheels turning and families eating. However, even distasteful drudgery can be redeemed if you remain committed to kingdom purposes. You may need to get realistic. Labor and pleasure aren't necessarily one and the same. Not all work is fun. Toilets must be scrubbed, letters must be typed, dishes must be washed, and papers must be written. But when you remember the larger purposes, the drudgery and monotony of your jobs are redeemable. For the Christian, kingdom purposes, goals and values must be number one. Read Matthew 6:33.

Three young men stood on the steps outside the Senate building in Washington, D.C., and looked out on the city. They saw the power that was there. They knew the significance of that place. But these young men prayed a simple prayer: God, we claim this city for you. We ask you to use us in your kingdom for whatever purposes you might have. We don't know how you will use us, but we are here to fulfill your purpose through us.

Richard Halverson went on to become the chaplain to the Senate, Doug Coe formed the National Day of Prayer in the nation's capital, and Abraham Verady went on to become a successful business leader. Because of their commitment to the kingdom, God used them to bring real power, real change, real vitality to that place.

Let's be honest. As college students you are the privileged of the world. If you persevere, you will graduate and move into positions of influence, authority and power. You will be teachers, executives, physicians, attorneys, pastors, nurses, artists, musicians, coaches and leaders in corporations, hospitals, schools, churches and endless organizations. You will help to shape those organizations through your decisions and values. You may not be the CEO, but you will be people who can make a kingdom difference in your work life. You will be parents to the next generation of children. With those privileges and with those opportunities are responsibilities given you by the Lord himself. Of the one to whom much is given, much is required. You will not move into those positions accidentally; God will place you there.

Not all Christian students get the job they want, but God intends to use all of you where you are placed. The question is, Will you remain focused on Jesus Christ and his kingdom, or will you settle for the lesser gods of profit, personal power and wealth? Your work is an opportunity to serve Jesus Christ and his kingdom. All of life—including your work life—is sacred, and its meaning is discovered in Jesus Christ. So whether you teach, run a bookstore, sweep floors and clean bathrooms, set policies and administer them, or type letters and manage an office, you do it for the Lord.

Therefore, you are accountable to God for the resources he gives you. As students you need to hold Christian faculty accountable for such commitment, excellence and devotion. And as long as you are a student, your studies are your work—there is no room for shoddiness, laziness and half-hearted commitment to your studies. Whatever you do, you do it for the Lord. We faculty and staff certainly will hold you accountable for such commitment, excellence and devotion.

I remember my first real job—I was a purveyor of goods at the Ice Cream Cart. That means I was a soda jerk. Unfortunately, I was a terrible counter person. I was incompetent with the menus, and I ate more than I sold. My boss never knew. And I didn't know about Colossians then.

My next job was on an assembly line. The first couple of days on the job, I tried to utilize the same standards I had set for myself at the Ice Cream Cart. Then old Bill, the line boss, came to me and to another student working at the packing end of the line. He looked at us and said, "Boys, if you're going to work for me, your work has to be better than good; it has to be your best." If a line boss in a tool factory can demand that, how much more do we owe Jesus, our real boss?

Discovering God's Will for My Vocation
Finally, Jessi and I talked about some practical ways to decide about a major and about a career. In *The Mustard Seed Conspiracy* Tom Sine outlines a series of steps that point the way to answers. I have adapted them into key questions.

1. What are God's intentions for the future, and how does God want

to use your life to further those intentions? What does God want to see happen in the world?

2. What areas of human suffering and need particularly grip your heart? Is Jesus calling you to serve through an area of your own interest and compassion?

3. In what areas have you experienced brokenness, and what are your gifts for kingdom service? God never wastes our experiences of suffering or of gifts. When you consider a major, you need to ask about areas of interest and delight. If you hated high-school chemistry and you're flunking Chemistry 101, a major in organic chemistry may not be a great idea! On the other hand, if you find yourself picking up books about social needs and you enjoyed your cultural studies course, perhaps a major in social work is something to consider.

4. What dreams do you have for the kingdom of God? Open yourself to dream big dreams and to surprising new ways of serving.

5. What do others who know you identify as your areas of strength? What can you learn from your own community of faith? What has your family told you that you always liked? Are there themes of interest that come back to you again and again? Ask your closest friends to tell you where they see you working in the future. Utilize the college career services office, and find out what career tests and inventories are available. Frederick Buechner described a "calling" as the place where your deep gladness and the world's deep hunger meet.

6. What does your experience of service tell you about God's calling? Experiment and try new ways of loving the world through compassionate service.

7. What can you hear in every dimension of life? God speaks in every part of our lives if we will pay attention. Use your common sense and think in very practical terms. What do events or even coincidences in your life suggest to you about a major or a career? Darrin was injured in a football game, but continued to love the sport. An opening for a videotape technician allowed him to stay near the game. As the season continued he found himself spending increased time in the video lab on campus. He now works in television.

Is there a magic formula? I wish there were. I could make a lot of money and reduce a lot of student frustration if I had one, but I think I might also keep people from some important listening.

Questions for Groups
1. What was your first real job?
2. What are your occupational goals at this time in your collegiate experience?
3. What difference would it make in your study life if you understood that Jesus is the boss and that studying is your job?
4. Pray for clarity about your future occupational choices.

23

Doc Martens, Espresso Makers, Jesus and the Mall

I remember the question because I knew the answer and did not want to admit it. "Aren't Christian students merely a reflection of the culture from which they come?" I knew what he meant by it. When he compared Christian students to secular students he didn't see much difference. Their clothes looked alike. Their music was often the same. Their values didn't seem much different either. Their spending patterns and tastes also looked surprisingly similar.

I had heard such a question before. When I was in Florido, a poor community outside Tijuana, Mexico, my new friends engaged me in a discussion about life on the other side of the border. The first question was intense: "How do you maintain your spiritual health in a culture that has so many things?" They understood the danger in a culture caught up in name-brand clothes, fast cars and the ever-present boom box. When it comes to the material benefits of our culture, Christians seem to blend into the culture easily.

Freshman Values

In 1970, 39.1 percent of freshmen surveyed had as a life goal "to be well off financially." By 1993 that number had soared to 74.5 percent! In 1970, 75.6 percent of freshmen had as a life goal to "develop a meaningful philosophy of life." In 1993 that number was 44.6 percent.

Jesus talks about money, material things and poverty/wealth more than almost any other topic. He is as concerned about how Christians handle wealth as he is about how they pray. Is your dream of a BMW a worthy goal for a Christian? Does Jesus have anything at all to say about Doc Martens, espresso makers and the mall? Luke 12 is a good place to begin.

Luke 12:13-31 is a troubling story. It cuts directly against the grain of all that people have been taught. Here is a man who was a model of success. He was a shrewd businessman, a wise farmer. He made good choices. He invested his time and energy well. And it all paid off for him. His land produced a good crop, which requires forethought and preparation. And he found that he needed to build larger storage silos for the bumper crop he had rightfully produced. This man would be welcomed on boards of directors for colleges, churches and civic organizations. He was, by normal American standards at least, a successful man. Why then does Jesus bring such a heavy judgment on the man? It almost sounds as if Jesus has something against success. Jesus' response is troubling.

The issue is, What is enough? How much do you need to be happy? What brings you satisfaction and contentment in life? How much? Where do you draw the line? What is enough? Jesus says two things that won't make any sense to you at first. I hope they do before you finish reading this chapter.

Some Is Not Enough

Where the farmer got into trouble was in his own mind, in his attitude and in his commitments. In essence, the farmer said, "I'll say to myself—to my soul—to my base of security—I'll say to myself: You have plenty of good things laid up for *many* years. Take life easy—eat, drink and be merry." He based his security on the abundance of his possessions. This disease of consumerism, which someone has called the "disease of more," has infected the American society in epidemic proportions.

That is why some is not enough. When we get some, we want more. At a profound level, material things do not have the capacity to provide satisfaction for the human spirit. When you confuse the two you end up empty, frustrated and dissatisfied. The farmer sat back and surveyed what he possessed—what he believed was the basis of his security—and he was fooled by the illusion of security. To this Jesus replied, "This very night your life will be demanded from you." Jesus was not against the rich. He was not opposed to private ownership, but he understood in a deeply profound way that some is not enough.

The fact of life is that everything is temporary. There are no promises, no guarantees of tomorrow. One evening I received a phone call telling me that my son was lying on a bed in a Philadelphia emergency room, and all the underpinnings of my life collapsed. In the time it takes for a phone call to be received or for a drunk driver to skid into your car, one's life can be changed dramatically. Life is fragile, and the things one believes are stable and certain can collapse in seconds! Just ask anyone in Southern California during the earthquakes that plague that part of the country!

The wealthy farmer in Luke confused means and ends. His possessions had become an ultimate, absolute end in themselves. They had become his god. That is why Jesus called him a fool. He was wise in the material realm but had ignored his own spirit. He was rich toward himself but impoverished toward God.

This is how Mother Teresa described citizens of the United States during a visit: "I have never seen such an impoverished people as the American people. They are building barns, but live spiritually in shacks."

One of the most radical messages of Christian faith comes into play right here. Christians need to understand very simply that life's primary goal has nothing to do with income, status, career or possessions.

It has nothing to do with power or position. The goal of your life is to become like Jesus Christ. Jesus says with great clarity: Set kingdom goals for your life. A Christian's goal is to build a sanctuary, a temple of the Holy Spirit, to bring your life to maturity in Christ.

I have a friend who is ruthless in his questions when we meet. He wants to know every time I see him if I am growing to maturity. He wants to know if I have taken seriously my task and set my goals high enough. He wants to know how I'm doing because he knows that I'm part of building something truly important—the kingdom of God.

Checkbook Checkup

Take out your checkbook right now. Take a look at your spending for the past thirty days. Look seriously at how much you spent in these categories: tuition, room and board, books. These are "necessary items." Now look at another category: pizza. I'm serious. How much money did you spend on eating out and on entertainment? This is "discretionary spending."

At a recent concert, the band asked us to consider giving fifty cents a day to support a child in a Third World setting. The next day I asked students at lunch what they thought about that. "Impossible! I could never afford that much! Are you kidding? I'm a poor college student." I wonder what the response would have been if I had asked them after they looked at their checkbooks. How would you answer?

Leo Tolstoy's remarkable short story "How Much Land Does a Man Need?" speaks volumes of wisdom. A Russian peasant had spent his life working another man's land. One day he heard of an offer being made by an enlightened nobleman. Peasants were given a chance to buy small parcels of land at an affordable price. The peasant quickly cashed in on this opportunity and bought a twenty-acre parcel. At last he was able to say, "This is mine!" It wasn't long, however, before he was no longer satisfied. He decided that he didn't own enough land. He heard about another province where land was cheap and easily acquired. So he turned his twenty acres into a down payment on two hundred acres and moved to the new site. Again he found himself restless. His excitement for this new parcel of land passed quickly, and he began to seek another purchase.

Finally he made friends with a wealthy man in still another province. This man made him a great offer: I will sell to you all the land you can walk around in a single day, all for only one thousand rubles. Totally intoxicated by this offer, he started out early the next morning. He began to drink in all that he saw, crying, "This is now mine, all mine." The farther he went, the greater became his desire to possess. He became so enraptured that he ignored the time. It was late afternoon when he began the long trek back. Panicked that he might lose it all, he pushed his body unmercifully to get back to the starting line. He ran as if his life depended on it and with the last glow of sunlight fading, fell exhausted at the starting point. As the people gathered around to greet this now wealthy landowner, they discovered that he had pushed too hard and had overtaxed his heart and died. At this point Tolstoy raises the question, How much land does a man need? The ironic answer is "Very little—a plot six feet long, three feet wide and four feet deep—just enough to bury him in" (in Leo Tolstoy, *Tales of Courage and Conflict*).

Jesus said, "A person's life does not consist in the abundance of his possessions." Some is not enough.

Enough Is Enough

In Luke 12 Jesus talks about the flowers in all their glory and the great value they have in God's sight. Most Christians are familiar with Jesus' words here: "Strive for his kingdom, and these things will be given to you as well" (v. 31). But he goes on to say, "Make purses for yourselves that do not wear out, an unfailing treasure in heaven, where no thief comes near and no moth destroys. For where you treasure is, there your heart will be also" (vv. 33-34).

That's the key. That's the answer to the question, What is enough? Enough is enough. Enough is all we need. Enough is found in a relationship with Jesus Christ. Seek first the kingdom. Seek your ultimate satisfaction in that which is ultimate. Seek your security in that which will not wear out or be exhausted, which no thief can steal and no moth can destroy. Give yourself to those things that are "big enough" and worthy enough for a son or daughter of the kingdom.

Jesus is saying something powerfully simple: Follow me—that's where you will find your satisfaction in life. You can worry all you want—it gets you nowhere. You can set your heart on money and possessions and watch a recession eat them up like a moth on a wool blanket. You can run after land like the peasant in Tolstoy's story and find that you'll get the same as everyone—just enough land for a cemetery plot.

Once again, however, Jesus' message doesn't tell you how to measure needs and wants. His words don't answer the question about a BMW. How am I supposed to know what to do? How do I judge what I need and what I want? Sometimes it seems like such a struggle.

There are tough choices to be made about money. Christians must ask themselves these questions.

Is your life committed to the task of making money? Then your life will be most impoverished. Is your life committed to the goal of reaching ever higher on the next rung of the corporate ladder? Then your life will be most misguided. Is your life given to the accumulation and possession of things—the best, the most, the newest? Then your life will take on an insipid taste and a never-ending search for more. The question of vocation is an important kingdom question.

How will you spend the money you earn? Will your income be given only to the pursuit of comfort? Or pleasure? An old saying sums it up well—enough is as good as a feast. One of the positive trends in Generation X is that some seem ready to accept a smaller paycheck in order to find values like serenity, relationships and family. It is time to find the freedom that comes from a righteous relationship with our possessions.

Enough is enough. That's not a formula, but it is a way of life. That's not a law, but it is a way of thinking. That's not an exact measuring stick, but it is a challenge. Seek first the kingdom. I don't have an easy answer that tells you how much is enough. I can't outline six questions that tell you how much to spend and how much to give away. Yet for most the answers are actually probably simple enough: you need to spend less and give away more. What I do know, however, is that Jesus intends for Christians to ask the questions, to take our discipleship to the mall.

Questions for Groups

1. What is your favorite possession, your most prized material possession? Why is it important to you?

2. What level of income is your goal for your future?

3. What did you discover about your spending habits from the checkbook checkup? What did you learn about your attitudes toward money?

4. Ask how you can pray for each other in the pressures of the week ahead.

24

It's About Time

Time is one of the greatest gifts you have been given. Someone once asked, "When you're lying on your deathbed, are you going to wish you'd spent more time at the office?" One of the most challenging questions you can ask yourself is, What does time mean in my life? Is it merely 60 seconds, 60 minutes, 24 hours, 7 days, 365 days multiplied by the number of years that you're given?

As I write this, a seventeen-year-old friend has just been killed in a motorcycle accident. His time was limited to 365 days multiplied times 17 years. What does time mean? Another student friend was involved in a truck accident that broke his back and left him in limited mobility for months. What does time mean? Yet another student friend was just diagnosed with cancer. What does time mean?

One of the most important lessons to be learned in college is how to value time. It is too easy to take for granted that time will always be available.

In a factory where I worked while in high school, a woman coworker would punch out every day and complain about wasting her day at work. Another coworker would always chide her for "wishing her life away."

Kurt Cobain, the lead singer of Nirvana, apparently concluded that time was too much, too pressing, too hard to continue—so he killed himself. His world, his success, his time became too much for him, and he ended it all.

But God's Word proclaims this truth: Time belongs to God. All of time is sacred. Time is a precious gift from God. God's command to "remember the sabbath day, and keep it holy" (Ex 20:8) is a reminder of these truths. What in the world does "sabbath" have to do with you and the world of college students? Many Christian students never darken the door of a church after they arrive on campus. Most students do not go to church on Sunday. Sabbath certainly doesn't mean that you worship time, but rather that you invest it wisely. Set your goals and your priorities and plan your use of time.

Walter Harrelson, author of *The Ten Commandments and Human Rights,* says,

> A community that recognizes that one day out of seven belongs to God and that the way to give it to God is to stop doing what one ordinarily does—break with the grasping for food and shelter and a better life, break with all efforts to secure one's place in the world, break with even the normal acts of cult and pilgrimage—such a community knows that life consists of more than work, more than food, more than shelter, more than protection from one's enemies, more than religious rites and sacrifice and prayer.

Time belongs to God—that's the essence of this commandment. So take time out. The sabbath should remind you that you're made for something bigger than working yourself to death, or worrying yourself to death, or running yourself to death for fear that you might miss something.

Pray and Play the Sabbath Away

The sabbath command is found in two places: Exodus and Deuteronomy. In Exodus the reason for the sabbath is to contemplate God. In Deuteronomy the purpose of the sabbath is social leisure or play. God seems to say, "Because you spent all that time in slavery—in hard and unrelenting work—you are to remember the sabbath." Pray *and* play. Joyful worship *and* holy leisure. The sabbath didn't start out merely as a day for religious activity, but as a day to stop the normal life of work and to celebrate, to rejoice. Holy leisure. Redemptive play.

The poet W. H. Auden says that people are in danger of losing their two most precious qualities: the ability to laugh heartily and the ability to pray. Sabbath-keeping involves both praying—getting in touch with your soul—and playing—laughing heartily, resting the soul from the frenzy and frantic pace of the work week. John Calvin filled his sabbath with both. In the morning he led his congregation in prayers, and in the afternoon he went among the people of Geneva and played a game called Skittles.

I will never forget standing at the western wall of the temple in Jerusalem one Friday afternoon about 5:00 p.m., the beginning of the sabbath. I wandered around as a tourist—looking, listening, fascinated to think that this wall was part of a temple that stood in Israel for many centuries. Then I heard the noise. It was a commotion at first, a disruption, a sharp punctuation of the quiet prayers and acts of worship going on by the crowds at the wall. The sound came from above and behind me. I looked up the street that comes down to the wall from another quarter of the city to see a large crowd of people—all men—coming my way. As they turned the corner and came down the hill, I realized that they were singing. Dozens of young men from the yeshiva, the Jewish seminary, were being led to the wall by an elderly rabbi, his wise face aglow with excitement. It was time for sabbath. Sundown on Friday. Time for faithful people to take time to let eternity in. Time to celebrate, to sing, to dance, to love God.

Soon I was caught up in a wonderful circle dance with hundreds of people who were there to pay attention to God. In that instant I knew what the psalmist meant when he said, "Make a joyful noise to the Lord." Why not? If I know who God is—the great Creator, giver of life, lover of people, lover of the earth—if I know who God is and who I am—a part of the covenant community of God—then how can I do other than rejoice with great passion?

Time Management on $4.00 Per Year
Jason held before me a gift from his dad. He looked at it with awe, respect and obvious delight.

"What is it?" I asked, although I already knew.

"It's my new planner," he said.

The Big Four

A friend asked me to describe how a college student could celebrate the sabbath. For me, it would include the "Big Four."

First, make time for worship. At Bethel College about five hundred students pack the gym at 10:00 every Sunday night for Vespers, a late-night, student-led time of singing, prayer and reflection. Many of the students say that Vespers is the right way for them to begin the week. They see it as a boost into the week ahead, a way to get ready for what will come by spending time in worship.

Second, make time for fellowship. Take time for relaxed enjoyment and fun. Take time to meet with people and to enjoy friends. Do some things that will make you laugh.

Third, make time for learning. Sunday-school classes, a Bible study and worship at your church all offer a way to renew the mind and to be transformed by it, as Paul says in Romans 12:1.

Finally, make time for service. Get up early on Saturday morning and volunteer with Habitat for Humanity, or be a big sister or big brother to a needy kid. You will find the rest of the weekend has a different feel if you give some time away to serve others.

Ask yourself: Do I approach the beginning of a new week with more serenity and joy than I felt at the end of the week? Think about how you spent last weekend and how it affected you as you headed into the rest of the week.

"How has it worked so far?" I asked.

I had heard this answer before. "Well, I haven't really gotten started yet, but my dad told me it will help me a lot!"

The ideas here are a lot cheaper than the $150.00 planner his dad sent.

First, buy a cheap weekly calendar. You might have to pay up to $4.00 for it, but you can also make your own. Work with a calendar that shows a week at a time. You need to see things from a weekly perspective. Some things will sneak up on you unless you keep the weekly view in mind.

Create a system that is simple and workable, something like the following:

☐ list all your classes
☐ list your work hours
☐ list your due dates for exams, papers and reading assignments
☐ list the holidays and breaks for the semester
☐ list midterm and final exams
☐ add Homecoming and other big events on your campus
☐ write in breakfast, lunch and dinner

These are the "givens." You don't have a lot of choices about these unless you choose to ignore them altogether. If so you'll have a lot of "free time" after the dean asks you to do your time management elsewhere. Then add the following:

☐ time every day for God (you decide how long and when, but write it in)
☐ time every week for physical exercise
☐ extracurricular activities and meeting times
☐ time every day for hanging out with your friends
☐ and, don't forget, time every day for *sleep*

Think about your values. Have you left time for relationships, rest, recreation, reading and music? If your list takes up more than twenty-four hours each day, you may want to cut back on some things. You can only do some things well. You have to decide which ones are important to you. You can wish someone will give you a formula for making up your mind, but don't believe it if you find one. You need to set your own priorities.

Some planners suggest that you think about the roles you play—such as student, son or daughter, worker, lab assistant, soccer player, Bible study leader—and then set goals for each of those roles every week. Be specific with your goals, such as:

1. Complete reading pages 54-112 of my lit text.
2. Write the first draft of my psychology paper.

3. Prepare a study guide for my physics class.

4. Read the passage for Wednesday's Bible study three times.

5. Write Mom a letter and mail it on Friday.

Some planners suggest that you set priorities in categories of urgent, high-priority, low-priority and "maybe next year."

Finally, remember this: you control your planner. Don't spend all of your time setting up and working with a planning system that takes up your valuable time. Use your planner every day and evaluate its effectiveness.

Jason bought a $4.00 campus planner with the important campus dates already printed for each week. For Christmas he plans to buy a $4.00 planner for his dad.

Questions for Groups

1. Create a calendar of activities for yourself from the past seven days. How did you spend your time? Use major categories like sleep, work, study, recreation, chores, hanging out.

2. What can you learn about your priorities from this calendar?

3. What does your group believe about the importance of sabbath in your weekly schedule?

4. Ask how you can pray for each other in the week ahead.

25

Majesty

I was on a backpack trip in the Cascade Mountains. We hiked about eight miles into the back country, passing fields of wildflowers, cooling ourselves from tiny rivulets that danced from the glaciers above on their journey to the rushing river below. We smelled the distinctive aroma of pine trees and drank in the forest green that literally and wonderfully surrounded us. We crossed over a glacial river and turned a corner in the forest—and what we saw took our breath away. In front of us was a four-hundred-foot waterfall careening down the mountainside, water dropping in sheets, power and energy and beauty all wrapped together.

I looked up and quite unintentionally said aloud, "Oh, Lord, my Lord, how majestic is your name in all the earth." Worship just happened. I didn't plan it, I didn't intend it, it just happened in a wonderful explosion of joy at God's majesty. Worship cannot always be like that, but we can learn to come to God with expectation and in anticipation that God will meet us.

Just Say Yes

In worship Christians say yes to God. Worship is the human part of the "phone call" that God has placed to humankind through creation and re-creation. It begins with an awareness that God has done something to which we want to applaud and say, Yes! God has created the heavens and the earth, and we say yes! God has given humans the opportunity for a re-created and reconciled relationship with him and with others, and we say yes! Worship begins with God.

In worship Christians say yes to the character of God. Worship is not something that we can make in our own image. In worship we recognize the character and nature of God. In worship we get our bearings and find our location in relationship to "true north." God is that magnetic center of the universe, and we acknowledge the very character of this God. In worship we say yes to God's holiness.

What is holiness? Stuart Briscoe once defined it as "something else." God is something else—something more and something other than we are. God is something else in purity and in excellence. God is something else in justice and in love. God is something else in majesty and creativity. God is something else in transcendence and power. God is something else in joy and the thrill of life. God is simply something else.

I once read a newspaper column about "the mush God," the God who shows up conveniently at political rallies and fraternal conventions to give an air of respectability and to help get votes. God then becomes whoever and whatever people want God to be. But the Old Testament says otherwise. In Isaiah God says in shocking words that not all worship is acceptable:

What to me is the multitude of your sacrifices?
    says the LORD. . . .
When you come to appear before me,
    who asked this from your hand?
    Trample my courts no more;
bringing offerings is futile;
    incense is an abomination to me.
New moon and sabbath and calling of convocation—
    I cannot endure solemn assemblies with iniquity.
Your new moons and your appointed festivals
    my soul hates;
they have become a burden to me,
    I am weary of bearing them.

When you stretch out your hands,
    I will hide my eyes from you;
even though you make many prayers,
    I will not listen;
    your hands are full of blood.
Wash yourselves; make yourselves clean;
    remove the evil of your doings
    from before my eyes;
cease to do evil,
    learn to do good;
seek justice,
    rescue the oppressed,
defend the orphan,
    plead for the widow. (1:11-17)

In Exodus God made it clear to the ancient people of Israel that they were not to make idols to worship. Why not? Because the God of the universe will not fit into a human image or idea. God is something else.

In worship Christians recognize who God, in reality, is. We meet the God who is, not the god we want God to be. Sometimes that means that we need to be transformed in worship. When Isaiah met God in the temple, his response was, "Woe is me! I am lost, for I am a man of unclean lips, and I live among a people of unclean lips" (6:5). He met God, and in the meeting, God changed Isaiah.

One day I got up in the middle of chapel and said in a stern, almost angry voice, "What are you doing?" People all over the chapel jumped. Some had been napping, some were "involved" with their friends next to them, and one even dropped a large textbook he was reading. I went on to say, "Do you realize the privilege we have this morning? Only a very small portion of colleges and universities take time out for their students and staff to spend time with Jesus. You wouldn't act this way in the presence of a visiting dignitary, a famous person or a celebrity, and I won't let you get away with doing it in the presence of the God of the universe!"

In worship Christians say yes to God's plans for us. Before Isaiah left the temple, he had a job to do—God was sending him out with a new agenda. God is free to do that. God is free to change and re-create our plans.

There once was a peasant girl whose name was Mary. She was a young teenager—fifteen or sixteen years old at most—who lived in the small town of Nazareth. She was waiting for her wedding day. She was engaged to a young carpenter named Joseph, and she no doubt felt that mixture of emotions that everyone feels—some hope, some fear, some excitement, some hesitation. This was basically a happy time for her. Her future looked bright and secure. Her parents had chosen carefully and had arranged well for her future. Something less than a year remained before she would take her place in Jewish society as a married woman. She was waiting.

But while she waited, her entire life was rearranged. For while she waited, the unexpected happened. A messenger of the Lord came to her and said, "Greetings, favored one! The Lord is with you." She didn't know for sure what that meant, but she was troubled by those words and by this interruption into her life. The messenger said, "Do not be afraid, Mary, for you have found favor with God. And now, you will conceive in your womb and bear a son, and you will name him Jesus" (Lk 1:28-31). I don't know if she heard the rest of the angel's words. But she did hear the first words: You will be pregnant, Mary, even though you have not had sex yet.

Can you feel the shattering, staggering blow this was for Mary? We'll never know all that she felt or thought, but she knew the reality of those words would change her world. For while she waited, God changed her life. While she waited, God changed her plans. God is free to change your plans too.

We had just completed our course on urban ministry in the city of Chicago. During the course we showed students the pain and deprivation of the inner city. We introduced them to some of the cream of God's church in people who faithfully and creatively serve God in inner-city neighborhoods. And we talked about the challenge of thinking about our place in God's kingdom, perhaps even in the ministry of the city. Students were sent off for a time of reflection about their answer to a tough question: To what is God calling you? After a while one of them came back and asked to talk to me. She was shaking and in tears. We sat down, and I began to probe.

What I heard caused me to have my own tears. "When I prayed, I suddenly began to think about my friends back home. I don't know why. I didn't want to think about them. I didn't plan to think about them, but I began to think about how I might be able to show them some of the God I have come to know here. I used to be afraid of that because I thought they might reject me if I became, you know, 'too religious,' but now I'm not afraid to go back home." And then she said in utter honesty and innocence, "Why did this happen to me? I have prayed many times before. I didn't really expect that anything would happen."

But something did happen: God met her there and empowered her and sent her off to her home with a vision for her life. God met her there in her time of prayer and worship and said to her, "Who will go for me?"

And she said, "Here I am. I will go."

Biblical worship will always include a time of sending forth. Go into your world and sing the song with great joy. Go into your campus and live the life with the greatest animation and excitement possible. Go where God asks you to go and answer, "Here I am. I will go."

Thou Art Worthy
Worship is the people of God coming together to attribute worth to God. The English word *worship* comes from a word that literally means worth-ship. To worship is to attribute worth to God in the community of God's people. You can still have personal and private times in which to do that. In fact, personal prayer times are needed and valuable. But Christians also need to come together to worship God. Much of the Old Testament includes instructions for how the whole people of Israel should conduct corporate worship. The experience of the early church included the consistent practice of worship-in-community. The book of Hebrews says, "And let us consider how to provoke one another to love and good deeds, not neglecting to meet together, as is the habit of some" (10:24-25).

A new revolution is beginning to rage all around us. Many people have rediscovered the great power in worship. New worship forms, new music and new media combined with the great liturgical traditions are creating a new day for worship. My dream is for some of you who read this book to find a vision for worship that will continue to reform and transform the church today.

My own involvement in ministry began when I criticized a worship service. That wise pastor asked me what I thought, and I told him. His response still stuns me today: "Well, Keith, since you have such definite ideas about what's wrong with our worship, will you be willing to help create and plan worship for next week?" My critical bluff was called, and I was drawn in. I began to ask myself all the right questions: What is truly biblical worship? What are the acts of worship that God seeks from people? How do we worship God as the whole people of God? What role does music play in worship? preaching? prayer? silence? Who is to lead in worship, and where does worship take place?

In the theaters of the past three groups of people were involved: the actors, the prompters and the audience. In much of contemporary worship in this country, the actors and prompters are the pastors and worship leaders, and the audience is the congregation. In biblical worship, however, God is the audience, the actors are the congregation, and the prompters are the worship leaders. Worship is not primarily a time of entertainment for the congregation-as-audience, but a time of actively participating in attributing worth to our God.

This leads to the final question: Did we attribute worth to God in our time of worship? Was our worship pleasing to the audience, to our God?

Joe came back from the summer with a joyful gleam in his eye. "I learned something incredible this summer," he said. "For a while I quit going to church. I didn't miss it much at first, but then I began to feel like I was going through my week half-asleep. I quit paying attention and I quit listening for God. But you know what? I missed the music, not the music at church only, but the music in my heart. When I quit going to worship, the music died inside. This summer I learned that I will run to worship if I have to because I have to have the music playing inside."

Day and night without ceasing they sing,
  "Holy, holy, holy,
  the Lord God the Almighty,
  who was and is and is to come." . . .
"You are worthy, our Lord and God,
  to receive glory and honor and power,
for you created all things,
  and by your will they existed and were created." (Rev 4:8, 11)

Questions for Groups

1. Describe your most recent experience of worship. Where was it? What was it like?

2. Describe your best experience of worship. Where was it? What made it spectacular?

3. Create a group description of the key elements of biblical worship. Read Isaiah 6 as a foundation for your description.

4. Spend time in worship together as a group. This doesn't need to be a long time, but try to utilize several of the key elements described above.

26

Let Me Help

*I*n the middle of a football game my friend Brett took a shot in the back as his body was extended for a pass. It didn't take long for everyone to realize that he was hurt, and possibly hurt badly. Along with the medical helpers who crowded around him were some of us who were there because he was a friend of ours. The entire Hubert H. Humphrey Metrodome was silent as the helpers did their work. There was a great witness to Jesus Christ as many prayed individually and then as the team gathered on the spot to pray for Brett.

Some of us wanted to help in some way, but we weren't sure what to do. And that's what I want you to think about next, the complex process of being a people-helper. Many people are motivated to help others, and may even get into the middle of things in their eagerness to help, but aren't sure what to do. To be a people-helper you must realize that helping is a sometimes complex process. But Jesus provides an example of how to be a helper.

John 5 tells of Jesus' encounter with a man who had been an invalid for years. He was dependent on the caregiving of others. Unable to work, unable to move freely, unable to walk, this was a broken man. The word *invalid* is pregnant with meaning, as it refers to that which disables someone, that which makes one in-valid. In this case the man's physical condition dominated his life, but his mental condition determined his world and made him invalid. Written across the days and nights of this man's world was the word *cannot.* His life was characterized by a constant no.

For many long years this invalid lived beside the pool of Bethesda, where many sick people gathered. Some believed that when those waters were stirred, angels of healing were standing by, ready to heal the affliction of the first one into the pool. And so from around the countryside they came, the blind, the lame, the physically afflicted. They would cluster around in the hope of being healed. What did Jesus do to help this man?

First, Jesus *saw* the man. How many times have I passed over a text like that? "When Jesus saw him lying there," he responded to him. He paid attention to him. Your acts of truest compassion begin when you notice the people who are there, when you see them, when you recognize them in their need.

One of the books that had a powerful impact on me as a college student was called *The Other America,* a book about the millions who live in poverty in this nation who are often not seen by the rest of us who are middle-class or wealthy. They are there all the time—but we don't see them. I used to work in Chicago and would take the commuter train through some of the worst ghetto areas of the city, but do you know what? The commuters were busily reading *The Wall Street Journal* or the stock reports and never once noticed what was there outside the window every single day.

But Jesus saw the man. Always he sees people who are invisible to everyone else. I love the chorus "Open our eyes Lord, we want to see Jesus"—but we cannot see Jesus in some highly spiritual, disembodied form. In Matthew 25 Jesus teaches his disciples how to see him. He will be seen in the hungry, the thirsty, the imprisoned, the poor, the needy. "When did we see you, Lord?" Jesus will answer, "When you acted with compassion for those in need."

God Give Us Tears
A few years ago I met John Perkins, one of the few true saints I've ever met. He was born in Mississippi, a sharecropper living in the squalor of poverty common to blacks in the Deep South during the 1930s and

1940s. He came to Christ at around age twenty-seven, when he lived in California and was just becoming successful. "Toop," as he was called, was starting to "make it"—good job, good pay, great future. During that time, however, he began to believe that Jesus wanted the world to be different for poor Southern blacks. Perkins was beaten and tortured nearly to death because he dared to return to Mississippi to take action for the sake of the poor. His life has been a shining beacon for compassion, racial reconciliation and practical love.

I attended a conference where John's wife, Vera Mae, gave a presentation. Vera Mae was talking about the needs of children in her community and in the world. She said something that has haunted my mind since then: "May God give us tears . . ." For her those were tears for the children of her community who are the greatest victims of poverty, racism and economic injustice. Where are the tears God wants to cry through you? For whom do you really feel the pain and the hurt and the brokenness that others experience?

When my friend went down in that football game, prayers were offered for him because we cared at that moment. Some of us even found tears in our eyes, heavy feelings in our chests and lumps in our throats. Yet some people need more than momentary attention. Some people need others to care enough to cry, and to take action on their behalf.

Do You Want to Be Made Well?

Jesus' second step in helping is that he approached the invalid with respect and freedom. He asked, "Do you want to be made well?" The question implies that the man had the freedom to refuse healing—to choose the status quo rather than growth. Jesus saw the man as an agent, as one with power and responsibility for his life. He treated him, as he treated the Samaritan woman, with dignity and respect.

Family therapists borrow a word from biology, *homeostasis*, which refers to the condition of a family that is stable and in equilibrium. It means that a family is living at a level of stability. But it can also refer to the choice that families will make to stay as they are—even if they are hurtful, abusive or contorted. In other words, sometimes people will choose the bad that is familiar rather than the new, because the new is scary.

Here was a man who became an invalid because he refused to stand and take responsibility for his life. Jesus cut through all of that with his question: Do you want to be made well? This must have seemed like the craziest question of all time. "Do I want to be well? Man, for thirty-eight years I have been unable to move without help, to go anyplace without help. I have no job, no future, no hope. Of course I want to be well."

But Jesus doesn't ask crazy questions. He understands that the human mind sometimes sees change as more terrifying even than suffering. So he asks, "Do you want to be made well?" Or have you become so accustomed to this way of life that you find it easier to stay here than to change?

The man at the pool refused to answer Jesus' question directly. He did what I suspect he had done most of his life—he gave an excuse. "Sir," he said, "I have no one to put me into the pool when the water is stirred up; and while I am making my way, someone else steps down ahead of me." It is an evasive answer at best, and a blaming answer at worst. "Lord, it's not my fault. Lord, what do you expect when I have the family I have? Every time I try to change, my roommate sabotages me. Lord, you don't know what it's like to be stuck like I'm stuck. Lord, I try, but everybody and everything is against me. It's not my fault."

But Jesus didn't accept his excuses and evasion any more than he accepts ours. He was not impressed that the man played the game of "pass the buck." He ignored his excuses altogether and called from him that which he calls forth from everyone every time we decide to take the risk of growth or change—he called for the man to act as agent, to be responsible for his life. There was no guarantee of his physical healing, but still Jesus put the issue of responsibility back into his lap: Are you willing to take the steps necessary to wholeness, are you willing to do what you can?

I once heard William Glasser ask a depressed person, "How long have you been depressed?" He then said, "The right answer is—long enough, because now I'm willing to take some steps to wholeness."

■ **Let Me Help**

The movie *The Mission* has an important lesson here. A slave hunter, a violent man driven by greed and untamed impulses and appetites, kills his brother in a fit of jealous anger. He is driven into immediate despair and is unable to forgive himself. A young priest enters his life and literally dares him to join his mission high above a waterfall at the top of a mountain. There is one condition, however—he must drag behind him an enormous netting containing the swords, helmets, armor and equipment of his past. He must ascend the steep mountain dragging these memories behind him. Often they drag him back down the mountain, erasing all the upward progress he has so painfully accomplished. More than once others in the party try to help him, to cut him free of his burden. But he always goes back and drags it up the mountain again. The image is powerful: he seems doomed to perpetually drag his past behind him, all the while it is pulling him down.

When he finally reaches the top of the precipitous peak, an Indian from the tribe he used to hunt for slaves approaches him with a knife in hand. There is a moment of dramatic uncertainty. Will this tribe avenge their many losses on this man? Is this his life—to drag his weapons behind him only to be killed and dropped over the side of the cliff? But no, the Indian cuts the rope and frees him from his overwhelming burden. And this time he lets it go, tumbling down the mountain back into the sea. Finally he receives forgiveness and is made well in that gracious act of love. The man has made a choice for growth. He has chosen wellness!

Jesus saw the invalid as a responsible agent—one with abilities and responsibilities for his own life. Jesus didn't come just to do *for* others; he came to empower them to take the next step for themselves. That is a principle for people-helping that resists codependency as it seeks to empower others to find their own strength.

Jesus saw the man, approached him with respect and freedom, and engaged the man as a partner in his own healing. "Jesus said to him, 'Stand up, take your mat and walk.'" He gave him the choice and waited to see what he would do.

Later Jesus said, "My Father is still working, and I also am working."

What does that mean? It means that you can introduce the personal power of God into every life situation. Someone once said it so clearly: "Ministry is introducing into whatever situation you find yourself, the God who is already there." The God who is still working. The ministry of caring is not a ministry of removing people's pain for them. You cannot. The ministry of caring is not a ministry to save anyone. You cannot. The ministry of caring is not a ministry of fixing the world for someone. You cannot. Rather, it is to see others with respect and freedom as agents, and to help them see the God who is there with them, working with them. This ministry is not merely a ministry of empowerment where you tell others to stand on their own; in Christian helping you tell them that they can stand because Jesus reaches out his hand and invites them to stand with him.

God wants you to be helpers and caregivers. But don't take away the other person's right to his own dignity and his own responsibility to suffer and to question, to stand before God in that awful moment of decision-making and then to choose whether to rise and walk or . . . or not.

One of my friends, a student named Mindy, had her leg amputated just above the knee because of complications from cancer. She went through difficult days of chemotherapy and recovery, of broken legs and surgery, and finally of adjustment to a prosthesis. As she told her story in our chapel one day, she talked about her friends. "I met a lot of good friends. Friends I knew God had given me. Friends I could tell my innermost thoughts to about how I was feeling and friends who I could pray with. These friends are very special to me. They were always there for me. They listened to me and gave me advice when I was going through another difficult time last year."

Her friends did many things for her, but they did not treat her like she was someone different. They listened to her, encouraged her, supported her and challenged her. Perhaps that's as good a definition of people-helping as you can get. I know some of her friends, and they are not people who want to create dependence. Instead they want to empower each other to growth and personal strength.

Caring is a complex thing. Jesus' kind of helping is to learn to see others, to see them as agents and then to help them see that God is a partner with them in their pain

Questions for Groups

1. Try to think back through the last twenty-four hours. Were there people in need around you whom you ignored, either intentionally or unintentionally?

2. What is your greatest difficulty with being a people-helper?

3. What brings you the greatest joy in being a people-helper?

4. Spend time helping each other to identify one quality of caring in each person in the group.

27

This Island Earth

Some years ago I sat in a meeting with Christian leaders from many churches in the Pacific Northwest. We were discussing the nuclear arms race and the response of the church to the proliferating buildup of those weapons of destruction. I argued rather vocally that we needed to be aggressive in our opposition to this military buildup, and one leader stood to counter my words. She said: "The church exists to save souls. The world exists only for the sake of man. The church needs to stick to its own business. After all, the earth will only last until Christ returns, whereupon he will destroy it. If we help to preserve the earth, we only delay the return of Jesus."

I sat in stunned silence as I listened to her image of a disposable, throwaway world. She was serious. And she illustrates what the church has been too slow to admit. The call to environmentalism has not come from the church, by and large, but from other sources such as the Sierra Club, the Audubon Society and Greenpeace.

Many in the church have that view of a throwaway earth. Since God will destroy the earth, why work to preserve it? This attitude has kept the church out of the environmental movement far too long. Fortunately, younger people today, college students especially, have joined the great environmental movement to save this island earth. In fact, an overwhelming majority of students today believe that the government still doesn't do enough to stop pollution in our nation.

Just the Facts

The average American family produces one hundred pounds of trash each week.

Last year Americans received more than sixty billion pieces of junk mail, or 230 unsolicited ads for every man, woman and child in the country. Although 44 percent of them remain unopened, the average American will spend eight months of his or her life opening junk mail.

Polystyrene foam is completely nonbiodegradable, which means that five hundred years from now the foam cup that held this morning's coffee could still be sitting on the earth's surface.

The environmental action groups call us to change on the basis of self-interest. We must take care of earth, our mother, or we will surely die. I want to offer a biblical perspective on this island earth, for Christians are called to environmental action as an act of obedient discipleship.

In Nature

Why should Christians care about the earth? To begin with, humanity is *in* nature. The writer of Genesis affirms that humankind and the earth share an essential oneness. Genesis 1:24-31 is the complete narrative of creation on the sixth day. In verses 24-25 God is at work creating the land animals. In verses 26-27 God creates people in his image. And in verse 31, "God saw everything that he had made, and indeed, it was very good."

All of life emerges from the source of God. That much is clear. Genesis tells us that both the earth and its human inhabitants come from the same source. Human life is somehow part of the earth creature by God. When God made the body of the man, he fashioned it from the dust of the earth. Before God breathed into this earthy creature, he fashioned him from the very soil of God's newly created earth. When God fashioned the body of the woman, it was from a rib that came from the creature who was fashioned from the dust of the earth. Elements of the earth are a constituent part of our physical makeup. When we die, we return to the dust of the earth.

In moments of deep philosophical thought, I sometimes turn to a favorite book compiled by David Heller: *Dear God, What Religion Were the Dinosaurs?* One ten-year-old boy asks, "Dear God, How long did it take you to make the first people? Do you feel you rushed too much?"

Larry, age nine, writes, "Dear God, Thanks for giving us the sky and the animals and the oceans. Thanks for new creations like computers. What will be your next item?"

Kenneth asks, "Do you consider Adam your son or is he like an invention?"

"Dear God, I love you so much. I love you all the time. When it is raining I feel so good about you. I also like the sun and the warmth and all the leaves in autumn and all the other wonderful creations you made. Everything but stuck up flirty girls." Signed Johnny, age ten.

Barbara, age nine, asks, "God, was the sky difficult to color? Did you consider anything else but blue? Maybe purple? Boy you must have been glad when you were finished coloring."

During the early years of the Christian church a teaching called Gnosticism emerged alongside Christianity. The Gnostics taught that humanity is a duality, that we are part matter and part spirit. But they went on to say that the body part—matter—was evil, because only that which is spirit is good. Therefore, they depreciated their bodies and all things material. They abused their bodies and misused matter. They lost sight of the value placed on matter in the Genesis account. They lost sight of this essential truth: humanity is in nature.

We are one with creation. G. K. Chesterton once said that Christianity is the most materialistic of all religions because of its creation doctrine. When God wanted to provide salvation, he didn't shrink from entering into human form. When Jesus returned after the resurrection, he came not as a disembodied spirit but in a glorified body. All of this says that there is a basic goodness to all of creation. Because God has created it, the earth has its own value, its own place, its own purpose. Humankind is to relate to nature according to God's design. We are in nature.

Over Nature

Humanity is also *over* nature. God says, "Be fruitful and increase in number; fill the earth and subdue it. Rule over the fish of the sea and the birds of the air and over every living creature that moves on the ground" (Gen 1:28 NIV). Another translation uses the phrase to "have dominion over." *Dominion* comes from the Latin word *dominus*. A dominus is a person who has taken mastery over a subject, has controlled it and has made it subservient. God has created people to be in nature but also to be over nature.

In Genesis 2 God gives Adam the responsibility of naming the animals. In the ancient world to name something meant to have control over it. "So out of the ground the LORD God formed every animal of the field and every bird of the air, and brought them to the man to see what he would call them; and whatever the man called every living creature, that was its name" (v. 19). The image here is not of Adam with a clipboard giving a label to each animal as they paraded by, but of the work of domesticating the animals. Adam learned to control and to master nature. Humans were created as workers. Even in the Garden of Eden there was a need for creative and responsible work.

Humans have been given responsibility for subduing the earth. We need to stop apologizing for finding ways to make our earth serve the needs of humanity. We needn't apologize for the progress that has been made in civilizing the earth and in bringing culture into the world. That is our God-given responsibility. We don't need to return to the frontier days!

On the other hand, the improper use of this responsibility has brought about the current ecological crisis. Whether it's the pollution of water supplies, the damage to the ozone layer and the air, or the destruction of rain forests, we have not been responsible in our "dominion-having." We have abused nature. That is not the divine order intended in creation. The real issue at stake here is responsibility—proper use of nature. Too often we have taken the attitude that "this earth is mine, I'll do what I please." Or, in the church, we have taken the view that only that which is spiritual counts. Thus we are guilty of our own forms of Gnosticism. When the church ignores damage done to the earth, we break a primeval law of God. And we contribute to what one writer has called an ecological Armageddon. We simply cannot go on forever abusing the resources of our basic support systems of air, water and the earth.

But as Christians we must understand that our motivation is theological, biblical and spiritual. We are not called to be environmentally concerned because this year is an anniversary of the original Earth Day. Christians are called to this concern because God's Word proclaims it.

People today have the attitude that they can do everything themselves. My own backyard offers a simple illustration of this independent attitude. My backyard is crisscrossed by electrical, telephone and TV cables. The electrical wires are tied to a pole and run across the yard in one direction. The phone company attached its wire in a different direction. Other wires and cables were added later, and they run helter-skelter in any direction.

I used to have a poster on my wall that showed a fractured world with the ecology logo superimposed. At the bottom the words read, "We have made a world for each of us. But we need a world for all of us." We were created to be in nature and over nature. Not as sovereigns who rule from afar. Not as destroyers who invade. But as those who rule in responsibility and mutuality as part of the very creation they are over.

Under God

Third, humanity is *under God*. The root of the ecological crisis is a faulty worldview. If our world had been created by chance, as some would argue, there could be no source of morality, of right and wrong, of responsibility. We would be left to our own designs. If the world had been created by an impersonal being, then we could treat ourselves and our world as impersonal things too. And these are two of the views that predominate in society.

Jewish philosopher Martin Buber says that there are basically only two ways to relate to everything. First is the I-it relationship, which sees no sense of mutuality between oneself and anything. There is no sense of oneness with anything, so a person is free to relate as subject with object, as "I" to an "it." One can manipulate, exploit and use anything in any way, for it has value only as a means to the ends of one's satisfaction. Humans have done this with nature, with disastrous results. The other way of relating is what Buber calls the I-Thou relationship. This way sees the mutuality and oneness that exists in all of life. It recognizes that all of life is a gift, God's good gift to us. One's task is therefore to relate with a sense of reverence and respect—out of a sense of belonging as part of God's creation. You are not to worship all things, but to accept their place in God's design. You are to respect God's purpose for their existence and treat all things with proper dignity. Humankind is to relate to nature according to God's design.

But what is God's design? We are in nature, we are over nature, and, finally, we are under God. The Christian reason for treating creation with respect is not simply that we're afraid we'll run out of natural resources in a few years, but that God is the sovereign Lord of the universe and has told us to. We are caretakers for the owner. April, age eleven, wrote this letter to God: "Dear Father, The earth is yours and every last thing in it. I want to say thanks for letting us rent it." Douglas Hall has argued powerfully that the question for this time in history is not "what will we do with God, but what will we do with God's earth."

Christians must affirm that all of life is God's good gift. The revolution is ablaze when you understand that everything you do is done as unto the Lord. If you recognize God's sovereignty over the earth, you will receive the earth's basic elements gratefully and use them wisely. You will value their richness and learn from them. You will stride into progress cautious of the delicate balances in the ecosystem.

A father gave his young son a map of the world that he had cut into many pieces. He hoped the puzzle would keep his child's attention for some time. Five minutes later the boy returned with the puzzle completed. His astonished father asked how he had done it so fast. "It was easy. On the other side was a man's picture. When I got the man together, the world was OK too." Simplistic? I don't think so.

A couple of years ago I participated in a tree planting at a college campus. After we put the trees in the ground, some of us did something I have never done before—we prayed for their growth. It was a moving time in which we expressed our trust in the God of tomorrow.

For indeed we don't own the future, we borrow it from those who will follow us. We hold it in trust for the Creator who asked us to watch it for him. We see it as a gift. We love it as part of our love for the Creator. We value it as God values this island earth. Almost 87 percent of freshmen in 1993 said that the government is not doing enough to control pollution (in A. W. Astin, W. S. Korn and E. R. Riggs, *The American Freshman: National Norms for Fall 1993*). My challenge for Christian college students echoes the words of President John F. Kennedy: Ask not what your government is doing about pollution, ask yourselves and your campus what you're doing about pollution. Please don't misunderstand me. The environmental crisis will not be resolved by recycling; it will be resolved only as all of us take our own responsibility seriously.

What Can I Do?

One of the valuable and very practical resources I know is the book *50 Ways You Can Help Save the Planet* by Tony Campolo and Gordon Aeschliman. Here are just a few of their ideas:

☐ Experiment with the thermostat. Turn down the heat.

☐ Settle for white paper instead of unrecyclable paper.

☐ Keep the oil changed in your car; it helps it run more efficiently.

☐ Take the lead at your school and workplace in recycling plastics.

☐ Buy a recharging unit and help to eliminate this nation's use of nonrechargeable batteries.

☐ Be a consumer who "writes the wrong" by informing companies about their environmental abuses.

☐ Just don't use the light when you don't have to.

Make it a personal priority to be a strong voice and advocate on your campus. Our campus has a strong recycling program. The four recycle bins are everywhere: one for cans, one for mixed paper, one for garbage and one for white paper. Yet every day I watch students drop everything into the bin marked "garbage." Every day I watch trays head for the dishroom full of wasted food and napkins.

You can save the planet, but it takes habits that begin now. It takes strong voices of students who will live with those habits and take the lead. Are you one of those people?

Questions for Groups
1. How do you react to Douglas Hall's statement above?
2. Who has most influenced your thinking about environmental issues and ecological living? What have they taught you about the environment?
3. Do you agree that our treatment of the earth is also a spiritual act?
4. Create your own top ten list of ways your campus can work to save the planet.

28
Two Kinds of People

*I*t has been said that there are two kinds of people in the world, those who believe that there are two kinds of people and those who don't. Tony Campolo would say that there are two kinds of Christians—those who admire Jesus and those who follow Jesus.

John Perkins had left Mississippi when his brother Clyde was shot to death by a white sheriff because he was making too much noise as he waited to see the Saturday-night show at the local theater. Perkins left believing that he would never go back to the racism, segregation and poverty of Mississippi. He had gotten out and was making it financially and socially in a new place. But in the midst of all of that Jesus spoke to him: Follow me. Follow me, John Perkins. Follow me. I want you to go back to Mississippi. I want you to show others my way. I want you to go back because I have a great work for you to do. You will take my name all across this nation.

Perkins said yes, but his wife Vera Mae was not ready to go. He became sick during that time, but God was working on Vera Mae's heart too. Finally she prayed, "Lord, it's a hard struggle for me to say yes, but I'm going to say yes. I'm willing to go. I don't want to go, but I'm willing to go. Lord, I'm going to say yes to you." After she prayed that prayer, a great burden was lifted from her. The great choking feeling she had had in her heart was gone. That prayer of surrender, after what had come as a hard command from God, ended up giving her real peace with God like she hadn't known for years (recounted in John Perkins, *Let Justice Roll Down*).

Follow me. It has less to do with what I want than with what God wants. Greatness is not found in achieving your own goals for yourself, your life and your career. It has to do with obedience to Jesus' words. Follow me.

Christians follow for one important reason—because God knows where he's going. The place is called the kingdom of God. Anything less than total commitment to Jesus and that kingdom is a sellout to lesser goals, to a lesser kingdom, to lesser gods. It's that simple! He says it: Follow me. He knows where he's going.

Dave Burdette is a missionary who followed Jesus to the mission field in Mexico. I met him when we took a missions trip to Tijuana with twenty college students. Few of us were ready for what we saw when we arrived. Florido was a shantytown of between 400,000 and 500,000 people living in 12′ x 12′ huts with no electricity, no running water, dirt floors and a latrine out back. Those with jobs had incomes of $2,000 a year.

A fire had destroyed the home of one woman we met. She was eight months pregnant and had been living basically under a tarp for several months. We built her a home—a space that is smaller than most of the bedrooms you will sleep in tonight. That is her whole house. Through a student interpreter, I talked to her about the honor it was to be there and the privilege I felt in meeting her. What I saw in her eyes was startling. I saw Jesus in her grateful eyes, just as she saw Jesus in our acts of compassion and caring. She said to me, "When you come back we will have a service in my home so we can give it back to Jesus for his use."

The Great Adventure, Revisited

You can follow Jesus on an adventure that is worthy of your time, or you can follow the culture around you—the crowd of opinion-makers at your school who decide what is cool, what is hot, who is in and who is out. If you choose the latter, you'd better ask yourself, "Do they know where they're going? Do you really want to go there with them?"

The United States has one of the highest suicide rates in the entire world. The drug use rate is also one of the highest in the world. Why is that true in a land of great wealth and privilege? It is true because the word of the day is conformity. People conform to the leaders, the opinion-makers who would lead us to be in the world and of the world too. Yet the truly exciting people I know in this world are those who have taken the risk and entered the adventure of following the cross.

Can you say to other people, "Come and follow me. I'm going somewhere you need to go"?

I read these words recently: "Make no small plans, for they have no power to stir the soul." I want to live my life that way—with big plans, big ideas, big dreams and big goals. Jesus has given me that when he said to go into all the world and preach the gospel. I have somewhere to go that is demanding, exacting, perhaps even dangerous, but it is worthy of my life—and yours. True leaders are those who want to lead people to worthy goals.

Do you remember Mark Twain's book *The Adventures of Huckleberry Finn?* Huck is hungry and sees a big loaf of bread floating along on the river. As he fishes it out and eats it, he decides that somebody like the widow or the parson must have been praying for him not to go hungry. But he concludes it would not work for him to pray, because prayer works for only the right kind.

It made me shiver. And I about made up my mind to pray, and see if I couldn't try to quit being the kind of boy I was and be better. So I kneeled down. But the words wouldn't come. Why wouldn't they? It warn't no use to try and hide it from Him Not from me, neither. I knowed very well why they wouldn't come. It was because my heart wasn't right; it was because I warn't square; it was because I was playing double. I was letting on to give up sin, but away inside of me I was holding on to the biggest one of all. I was trying to make my mouth say I would do the right thing and clean thing . . . but deep down in me I knowed it was a lie, and He knowed it. You can't pray a lie—I found that out.

Huck knew that there had to be integrity between his words and his life. This is what others will notice about you. Do your words and actions work together?

If you've been on campus for a while, you know that a Christian

---

Integrity Inventory

Am I honest in my use of time on the job? Do I give a full hour's work for every hour paid? (Even if "it's only a work-study job.")

Am I truthful in my words to other people?

Am I honest in my classwork and papers? Do I avoid the opportunity to cheat on a test or paper?

Have I learned the fine art of integrity with my parents and family? Do I tell them the truth about myself and my life?

Have I learned to speak the truth in love?

---

college is not a bubble of perfect spirituality and integrity. Most Christian colleges have a lifestyle statement, a pledge, a list of community rules. Most of them focus on the same things: alcohol use, sexual behaviors, tobacco use, honesty and so forth. Many students have signed these lifestyle statements or pledges of behaviors. At stake in all of these documents is the word *integrity*. Integrity means, very simply, "what you see is what you get." If you agreed that you would follow those guidelines, what's on the line is your own integrity. You may not agree with every part of the lifestyle statement and may not intend to live this way after commencement, but as long as you are a student, your word is on the line. Does your word stand up in the light of day? Or does it crumble when the light strikes it, revealing all the cracks and flaws in it?

Paul is very clear on this point. "Whatever you do, in word or deed, do everything in the name of the Lord Jesus, giving thanks to God the Father through him" (Col 3:17).

Questions for Groups

1. Which part of the integrity inventory was most revealing? Tell the group about it.

2. Create a group definition of *integrity*.

3. What hinders us from living as people of integrity? Discuss this with the group.

4. Create a group covenant of mutual accountability for one area of personal integrity.

29

Your Mind Matters

It was a strategic moment in the weekend retreat at Inspiration Hills. "Captain Campfire," Steve Young, was back in town for another commitment. In his absence Jeff and I strapped on guitars and strode courageously to the front to lead the restless students in singing.

The first song came to an abrupt halt when the would-be song leaders discovered that we couldn't play some of the chords. We tried another song, but no one would join in the singing. And then we discovered a song that both of us could play—it had only three basic chords played in repetition. The song was "Thinkin' . . ." You may know how the song goes: "Thinkin' . . . thinkin' . . . thinkin' about thinkin' . . . thinkin' about thinkin' in my song, tell it to the people as you pass along, thinkin' . . . about thinkin' . . ." There we were, Nelson and Anderson, about to begin a new career in music. Then we got to the part where the song leaders ask what people are thinkin' about. "What are you thinkin' about, Paul?" The reply from the back of the room was, "I'm thinkin' about singing a different song."

I sat down once with a current bestselling book that featured devotional thoughts for the whole year. I started scanning its pages for its words about thinking. But there wasn't a single reference to thinking in that entire book! And I find that to be a scary fact. For you see, how we use our minds is absolutely critical to our growth in Jesus Christ. Students especially need to comprehend this fact. Jesus instructed his followers to love God with their heart and soul, that we know. But sometimes we forget that we are also instructed to love God with our minds.

In Philippians 4:8-9 Paul deals with the question of matters of the mind. How do we use our minds? Paul deems that an important concern. He knew that there were many forces and influences on the people in Philippi, just as there are on us. His people were being subjected to many different ideas and teachings and philosophies. Many religions and many values were crying for the minds of his people.

Commercial television is full of programs that compete for your attention. But the goal of television is neither information nor entertainment. It is not primarily about news or culture. Rather, its primary goal is to create a marketplace, a place where consumers and advertisers can meet. We understand that. Everybody is selling us something. Most serious of all, perhaps, is the subtlety of the selling of values to our minds. As they seek to create that marketplace, they also begin to shape our thinking and quietly change our values. You just sit down to zone out, you think, and all the while you are taking in the viewpoints, ethics, values and ideas of the culture. And of course this is true of the music you listen to, some of you around the clock.

Instead I want to look at Paul's criteria for evaluating how to use our minds. He left a series of demanding tests for what we think about.

Thinking About Thinking

Paul lists seven principles for the early Christians to use as a measuring stick against first-century culture.

First, Paul wants the believer to ask, *Is it true?* Is it consistent with reality? Is it real? Is there integrity in this? You must question much of what comes at you today. It may be convenient or accepted by society, but it may also be a distortion of God's truth. It may take life and make something of it that God never intended.

In the Acts of the Apostles the story of Ananias and Sapphira is a clear illustration of this. Barnabas was moved by God to sell his property and share the proceeds with those in need in the city of Jerusalem.

Later Ananias and Sapphira, also Christians, sold a piece of their property. That was consistent with what Barnabas did. But they kept back part of the proceeds from the sale. When Peter asked them if this was all of the money, they answered yes. Peter could see that the truth was not in those words and confronted them, saying, "You did not lie to us but to God" (Acts 5:4).

Paul urges us to think about that which is true, that which is real and honest, not phony and plastic. To discover what is true and what is distorted requires some disciplined thinking. It means that you don't just take in whatever words are pushed your way and accept them as equally valid. It means that you must develop an ability to discriminate between truth and lie, truth and distortion.

One writer says Christians must always ask, "Is my perception of _____ realistic in light of the gospel? Is it consistent with what I know to be true in Jesus Christ?" This assumes that you will know the mind of Christ through your study of God's Word. In his book *The Hebrew Scriptures*, Samuel Sandmel observes: "More people praise the Bible than read it. More read it than understand it, and more understand it than conscientiously follow it." We must always come back to the standard of truth in Christ.

The second test asks, *Is it honorable?* Simply put, is it worthy of your time? In the ancient world the word used here referred to that which had the dignity of holiness on it. When you spend your time with something, you are reverencing it. You dignify it by your attention. At times you need to do that in order to critique something and to develop your thinking skills. But how much of the time are you like a sponge soaking it all in, taking it all in without giving it a second thought?

Perhaps an alternate way of asking this is to ask whether you spend too much of your time with trivial pursuits. Giving your precious minutes and hours to the pursuit of the trivia society creates is a serious spiritual issue. Our lives have only so many minutes and hours. How are you choosing to spend them? What do you allow to fill your mind, your thoughts, your imagination? Paul asks, is it honorable?

Next, *Is it just?* Is it righteous? Is it moral and upright? William

Barclay says that the Greeks described the righteous person as the one who gave to the gods and to other persons that which was their due. Are you filling your mind with input that will encourage you to give to God and to others their due? One writer calls this the principle of "the right as opposed to the convenient." So much of what we hear and see and think about is based on the convenient, the easy, the pleasurable, the selfish. "I try to find the easiest, most pleasurable way to get what I want. And if I step on others in the process, that is their loss; I need to take care of me and mine."

But Paul asks, "Are you filling your mind with ideas that will lead you to see that justice is done in the world? Or have you learned no longer to see the hurts and pain and injustice in our world?"

I was moved by this account from a court translator. He called it "Justice? Don't Bank on It."

He was a broken middle-aged man. His feet were bare, his back was hunched. Above all, I remember his eyes: fearfully wide open like a wounded puppy, unable to comprehend the disaster which had befallen him. He was in jail. He spoke no English. If eyes were the window to the soul, then surely his soul was terror stricken.

His crime? Overdrawn bank account. How much? $50. The time? May 1977. The place? Wichita, Kansas.

A bank account which is overdrawn by $50 or more is not just a misdemeanor here, it is a felony. So the man was arrested. As an elementary courtesy, I requested to meet him before the formal court session. They took me to the holding pen where I spoke to him briefly through the bars. For only introducing myself in Vietnamese, he thanked me again and again.

A few minutes later I stood by his side to translate the one-way communication as the judge read the indictment and the procedure for obtaining a defense attorney. After an attorney was appointed, the Vietnamese man was whisked away. I may never see him again.

But then he interprets his experience: "I may never see him again, but I'll never forget those eyes. Sometimes I wonder where justice is, especially when I reflect on the top leadership of the United

States just a few years ago." Perhaps Kahlil Gibran was right after all when he wrote, "The net of the law was devised to catch small criminals only." Is it just?

Fourth, *Is it pure?* Morally pure? Something that is pure is not stained or defiled. Will these thoughts stand the scrutiny of God?

Think about the morality preached in the music you hear every day. Think of the ethic of selfishness preached through every form of media around. Society asks, Do you want it? Then grab it. Paul asks, is it pure?

God's purpose isn't to restrict you from everything fun. But if you simply capitulate to the standards of society for your relationships, your goals, your values and your ideas, then you have given yourself over to much that will never stand up to God's scrutiny. God's Word is not a handbook of ethics, but it certainly points to the target of God's intentions. Never forget that God has set standards of righteousness and purity for all.

Jesus said to his followers, and he says to us, "You are the light of the world. A city set on a hill cannot be hid. You are the salt of the earth." Christians are here to shine and to flavor the world and its values. Jesus didn't tell his followers to go into all the world and blend into whatever they find. He said, "Go and make disciples . . . teaching them to obey everything that I have commanded you" (Mt 28:19-20). We need a continual intake of the purity of God's teachings.

The fifth test is, *Is it pleasing or worthy of love?* Literally, does it promote sisterly and brotherly love? Does it serve to bring people into harmony and unity, or does it add to the friction and discord that eat away at human relationships?

Sixth: *Is it commendable?* That is, is it of good report and gracious? Another translation says to think about "whatever has a good name." One writer said, "It might not be going too far to say that it describes the things which are fit for God to hear." If God were listening to your conversation, would he be pleased?

Finally, Paul says, *"If anything is excellent or praiseworthy—think about such things"* (NIV). Whatever is worthy of praise.

Is it true, honorable, just, pure, pleasing or worthy of love, commendable, worthy of praise? Think about these things.

Questions for Groups

1. Create a paraphrase of each of Paul's seven principles.

2. Select a burning issue on your campus and use the seven principles Paul has given us to decide what your response should be.

3. Which of the seven principles is hardest for you at this time in your life?

4. Commit yourself to developing integrity in one of these principle areas. Pray for each other as you make this commitment.

30

Don't Forget

A ny step into tomorrow begins with an ending—you say goodby to what has been, and then you say hello to that which is new.

I once asked a student what I should preach in the final chapel service of the year, and she said to give them something simple to remember all summer long. Jesus did that when he sat down with the disciples as they prepared to finish their time together. He gave them three things to remember.

First, remember to learn. For three years Jesus had taught the disciples about the kingdom of God. In his last days with them he continued to do the same thing. He taught them about how God must become the central focus of one's life, about learning to rebuild the world as a new kingdom of truth and justice and love.

For some students, summer is a time to take the brain out of the skull and put it on the shelf, to give it a rest, to "veg out" and simply not do the hard work of thinking. But please don't do that. Your education in the faith is not yet complete. That's good news. Life in the kingdom is like that—it's not a matter of "doing it rignt" or "doing enough." Kingdom living is a matter of a relationship with the Ruler of the kingdom.

Calvin and Hobbes are good friends of mine. I love to enter the world of Calvin, who is able to re-create the world around him, to see it differently in his imagination from the way it is in flesh and blood.

In one adventure the two of them are hiding in a tree because they pushed the family car down the driveway and lost control of it.

His mother spots him in the tree. "There you are, come down so I can talk to you."

"No, you'll kill us. We're running away."

"I'm not going to kill you," his mother reassures him. "I just want to find out what happened. Are you okay? Was anyone hurt?"

"No," Calvin replies. "No one was hurt. We were pushing the car into the driveway and it kept rolling. It went across the road into the ditch. That's when we took off."

"Well, the tow truck pulled it out and there's no damage," she says, holding out her arms, "so you can come home now."

"First," says Calvin, peeking his head around the tree trunk, "let me hear you say you love me."

This is the heart of the kingdom of God—Jesus says, I do love you. I love you even though you pushed the car into the ditch. I love you. I want to build a bridge for you to God. It's a bridge of love. So remember to learn about the kingdom of God.

Second, remember to listen. Jesus told the disciples to go to Jerusalem and wait for the Holy Spirit to arrive. They were to listen for God's voice and God's power to appear.

God will speak to your heart if you wait and listen. For several weeks about eighteen guys met on Wednesday evenings. The format was very simple—one or two guys volunteered to listen to whatever God would bring to them, and the following week they shared that word—and there were powerful times of hearing God's messages.

Listen for the voice of God.

Listen for the voice of truth in your own questions and struggles.

Listen for God to speak through the Word.

Listen for God to speak when you pray.

Listen for God when you worship.

Listen too for God to speak in the voices of the poor, the dispossessed, the oppressed. Whether they speak from Bosnia or South L.A., from Minneapolis or Central America, listen to those who have been oppressed. God speaks in many ways.

Third, remember to serve. Jesus said to the Twelve, "You will be my witnesses." I am always moved by Francis of Assisi's profound words "Always remember to preach the gospel, and if necessary, use words." Summer is not only a time to kick back and relax in the sun. Go. Serve.

Say Thank You and Goodby

For his last time to address students in a chapel service, a professor gave the following message, entitled "My Last Lecture":

Tonight, the nail is peeled from a young black
thumb in South Africa. You know that. Tomorrow
in Argentina mothers gather again in the plaza
to weep, fathers
of a thousand children lie blistered, bludgeoned
in a ditch. You have ears to hear them weeping
now. Just when you thought you could answer
you hear the drone of huge planes lifting
into a California sky the color of blue steel
holding in their bellies the end
to your children. No more babies. No more
swallows come back to the eaves. No more bodies,
sweat of hands, thrill of necks, no more
love. Tonight you wonder at the price
of knowing, knowing
you have come this far, you will
never turn away.

But your family waits in Portland to hear. Your mother
waits in Tucson for comfort. And how
to tell them. You are not the girl who wanted
just to please. You are not the boy
who wanted football more than understanding.
How to tell them Jesus isn't easy.

How to tell them you are afraid.
You feel as fragile as a daffodil whipped by a raw
spring wind. You blossom
but all the while you tremble in the cold, dark air.

Listen. For the last time I have something
to tell you. I want to tell you
what I know. I know very little
but I know the sun rose this morning
like a huge torch. I know the flesh
is sometimes sweet. When you are held
in someone's arms, those are the arms
of God. I want to tell you I saw the plum tree blossom
once again, swallows flash their bright green wings
over the river. I want to tell you I believe
very little, but I believe the lamb
takes away the sin of the world. A lamb,
think about it, the sin of the world.

It's time to leave. Leaving is not easy.
And what can I tell you?
Your friends will die. You will love them hard
and still they will leave. Just when you think
you know how to soothe the world's weeping, your words
will taste like ash, your wisdom will turn an empty husk.
Someday your mother will grow weary, someday
you will hold your son, sobbing, frightened,
and you will know pain deeper than living.
So what can I tell you?
Learn the names of flowers.
Learn again and again, how to hold someone's hand.
Learn how to carry a candle when the night winds are blowing.

And learn how to say thank you and goodbye. (Phil Eaton, in
Today 55 [September 1985]. Used by permission.)

Fragile Memories

Some of us are very good at embellishing memories. It may have been Mark Twain who said, "The best memories I have are of things that never happened." Some of your best college memories will be like that. They get so much better as time goes on that no one else will remember them quite the way you do.

And, of course, different people remember the same event in different ways. All throughout my childhood, my Uncle Harry loved to tell a story about me. Harry was a housepainter and was working on the front of our house when I was about five. He was using the garage as his base of operations and stored paint there before transferring it to the can on his ladder. When he went to the garage at one point he found paint splattered all over the floor and dripping down the can. He screamed my name, and I came running. He looked at my hands and shirt and found . . . nothing. So for years he told this story about how clever and devious I was to spill the paint without spilling any on myself.

One Christmas a few years ago we were telling that story again. I admitted that I did not remember the event except from the continual telling of it. Then my older sister suddenly got a huge grin on her face. And then and there she confessed—some thirty years later—that she was the one who had spilled the paint.

Memory. Telling the great stories. We need to do that.

Elie Wiesel, the Jewish recorder of the Holocaust, tells the story of the Jews of the Hungarian town of Sighet who were rounded up and deported to concentration camps in 1944. Wiesel was one of them. He survived the Holocaust and returned home twenty years later. What pained him most of all was that the people of Sighet had erased the Jews from their memory. He writes, "I was not angry with the people of Sighet . . . for having driven out their neighbors of yesterday, nor for having denied them. If I was angry at all it was for having forgotten them. So quickly, so completely . . . Jews had been driven not only out of town, but out of time as well."

Basic Facts to Remember

First, *don't forget who you are.*

So if anyone is in Christ, there is a new creation; everything old has passed away; see, everything has become new! (2 Cor 5:17)

He was in the world, and the world came into being through him; yet the world did not know him. He came to what was his own, and his own people did not accept him. But to all who received him, who believed in his name, he gave power to become children of God. (Jn 1:10-12)

This is my commandment, that you love one another as I have loved you. No one has greater love than this, to lay down one's life for one's friends. You are my friends if you do what I command you. I do not call you servants any longer, because the servant does not know what the master is doing; but I have called you friends, because I have made known to you everything that I have heard from my Father. You did not choose me but I chose you. (Jn 15:12-16)

As the Father has loved me, so have I loved you. (Jn 15:9)

You are God's loved ones. You are women and men chosen, called, appointed, commissioned, empowered, sent, adopted, embraced by the Lord Jesus Christ.

Second, *don't forget where you're going.* Every spring I talk to college seniors who look to the future with uncertainty and some fear. Many of them are concerned about careers, about finding a job, about paying their debts. One senior asked me, "What am I going to be when I grow up? What career should I have? What am I going to do with my life? Where am I going with my future?" The questions were many—the concern was high.

Finally, I said to her, "It doesn't matter ultimately what you choose to do with your career and your vocation; what matters is not what you will *do,* but who you will *be.*"

My hope for you is that you will prize the kingdom of God as you look to your future. Decide who you want to be in the fall, or a year from now, or even five years from now. What values will guide your summer and the rest of your life? What relationships will be most important? What will be your dominant goals? What will drive you? I know that you need to make some practical decisions too, but don't let those decisions cause you to lose sight of the more basic issue of where you're going in Jesus Christ.

You are remade into the image of your goals. That is why Jesus was so brutally clear when he told his disciples to seek first the kingdom of God. Don't set anything else in that place of priority. That's why God told the people of Israel that the first commandment is "I am the LORD your God. . . . You shall have no other gods before me." That's why Jesus told his followers to love the Lord their God with all their heart, all their mind, all their strength. Love God with head and heart and hand—with what you think, with what you value and with what you do.

Don't forget who you are. Don't forget where you're going in Jesus Christ.

Questions for Groups

1. What goals can you set for the next months?
What will it take to achieve those goals?

2. Go around the circle and tell each person one great contribution they have made to the group.

3. What has been the greatest gift of this group to your life?

4. What answers to prayer has your group experienced? List several of those prayers. Pray for each person by name, asking God to help each one in his or her future plans.

For Further Reading

The Church
Campolo, Tony. *Wake Up America!* San Francisco: Harper & Row, 1991.
Colson, Charles. *The Body.* Dallas: Word, 1992.
Sine, Tom. *The Mustard Seed Conspiracy.* Waco, Tex.: Word, 1981.
Snyder, Howard. *A Kingdom Manifesto.* Downers Grove, Ill.: InterVarsity Press, 1985.
Stott, John. *The Contemporary Christian.* Downers Grove, Ill.: InterVarsity Press, 1994.
Webber, Robert E., and Rodney Clapp. *People of the Truth.* New York: Harper & Row, 1988.

Developing a Christian Worldview
Boice, James Montgomery. *Foundations of the Christian Faith.* Downers Grove, Ill.: InterVarsity Press, 1986.
Evans, C. Stephen. *The Quest for Faith.* Downers Grove, Ill.: InterVarsity Press, 1986.
Gill, David. *The Opening of the Christian Mind.* Downers Grove, Ill.: InterVarsity Press, 1989.
Sire, James. *Discipleship of the Mind.* Downers Grove, Ill.: InterVarsity Press, 1990.
_____. *The Universe Next Door.* Downers Grove, Ill.: InterVarsity Press, 1988.
_____. *Why Should Anyone Believe Anything at All?* Downers Grove, Ill.: InterVarsity Press, 1994.

Marriage
Hybels, Bill, and Lynne Hybels. *Fit to Be Tied.* Grand Rapids: Zondervan, 1991.
Smith, M. Blaine. *Should I Get Married?* Downers Grove, Ill.: InterVarsity Press, 1990.